STEVENS' POETRY OF THOUGHT

Theoretically, the poetry of thought should be the supreme poetry . . . . A poem in which the poet has chosen for his subject a philosophic theme should result in the poem of poems. That the wing of poetry should also be the rushing wing of meaning seems to be an extreme aesthetic good; and so in time and perhaps, in other politics, it may come to be.

—*Stevens*, "A COLLECT OF PHILOSOPHY"

STEVENS'
POETRY OF THOUGHT

BY FRANK DOGGETT

THE JOHNS HOPKINS PRESS
Baltimore

FOR DOROTHY EMERSON
who collaborated in every aspect of this
book except the actual writing of it.

≼⁽⬚⬚⬚⬚⬚ PREFACE ⬚⬚⬚⬚⬚⬚≽

The rising and setting of the sun are for most men at most times, as Stevens observes, no more than the meaningless recurrence of the quotidian. For only a few minds will the event gain import and the idea of "the universe of space"[1] or of "the infinity of the world" or some other interpreting concept be realized. In "A Collect of Philosophy" Stevens maintains that simple concepts of this kind—and by *concept* he seems to mean an idea married to an image—are the common ground of philosophy and poetry. He states a preference for poetic concepts that give "the imagination sudden life," and he finds them best expressed by a philosophic mind "to which metaphor is native and inescapable, which chooses to make its metaphors plain, and thinks from the true abundance of its thought." This characterization reveals his quite natural inclination for philosophic writing that uses imagery like his own and offers concepts with intricate possibilities for contemplation, like those of his own poems.[2] By way of illustration, he quotes from Jowett's introduction to the *Phaedo* a sentence whose conjunction of concept and imagery is appropriate for a poetic concept: "Is the soul related to the body as sight to the eye, or as the boatman to his boat?"

[1] Unless otherwise noted, all quotations in the Preface are from "A Collect of Philosophy," *Opus Posthumous* (New York, 1957), hereafter cited as *OP*.

[2] Stevens' interest in the poetic concepts of philosophers is one that Lovejoy finds shared by philosophers as well as those who read philosophy for literary purposes. His term for the poetic element in philosophy is "metaphysical pathos." *The Great Chain of Being* (Cambridge, 1957), pp. 10–14.

"A Collect of Philosophy" is evidence of a long search for concepts that are seeds of feeling and thought and that are easily transplanted into the language of Stevens' poetry. Comparing the sudden realization of a concept holding large philosophic possibilities to the germinal concept of a poem, he describes the evocative power of both for their own purposes. The philosophic idea, he says, sometimes appears "effortlessly and as a whole, as distinct from its details, in the same way that the gist of a poem comes into the poet's mind and takes possession of it." Like the poet the philosopher has the habit of forming concepts, and a philosophic concept is often a spontaneous imaginative insight that seems to come from "the same miraculous shortenings of mental processes that the poet experiences." And like the concepts out of which poems grow—the kinds of poems described by his phrase "the poetry of thought"—the concepts of philosophers are often "triumphs of the imagination."

This may all be quite naïve to a student of philosophy, but it reveals to the student of Stevens the importance of philosophic concepts to his poetry, especially his impression that such a concept may be the occasion of a poem. It shows that in his view a concept could hold inherent aesthetic possibilities, could become an object of contemplation, and could evoke an inner discourse and echoing feeling. He remarks that the distinction between feeling and thought vanishes at the inception of a poetic concept and says that "in the excitement of bringing things about it is not always easy to say whether one is thinking or feeling or doing both at the same time." A poetic concept at work in a poem of Stevens is a nucleus of possibility, an undeveloped implication, as free of dialectic as an image.

The concepts that emerge from long reading of the poetry of Stevens are so slight and so basic that any elementary course in philosophy or even a few years of interested reading could yield all of them; yet, these concepts taken together are not mere miscellaneous samplings, for there is an accordance among them. The accordance is probably a result of Stevens' preference for naturalistic thought and for ideas that lean on the imagery of organism. Also, the concepts have been given a new birth in the poet's mind and language and emerge with his own distinctive features. Still, there is no dialectic to support them, and they never cohere into an organized body of thought. In general, throughout Stevens' poetry, the only continuous strand of thought is a fundamental naturalism that is immediately apparent in the poems of *Harmonium*. This naturalism is as much a sentiment, as much an expression of an allegiance—a piety and an affection —as it is an expression of thought. The allegiance is to earth, and the sentiment is expressed in many celebrations of the reality that is the substance and support of his existence.

The concepts that are submerged in Stevens' poetry are usually some variation of the idea of the subject-object relationship[3]—what Stevens so often refers to as "the interrelation between reality and the imagination" that he says is "the basis of the character of literature." The phrases are from the only published exegesis by Stevens of one of his own poems, "A Note on 'Les Plus Belles Pages.' " The significant thing about this exegesis is that in it he explains the meaning of the poem in terms of a concept. "Apparently," he begins, "the poem means . . .," and he mentions the specific objects of the poem, its nouns and the overt statement about them. "What it really means is that . . .," and he tells the real meaning in terms of an idea. For the critic of Stevens, it is of paramount importance to notice that the poet sees an idea

---

[3] For a discussion of the subject-object relationship as the major theme of Stevens' poetry, see Roy Harvey Pearce, "Wallace Stevens: The Last Lesson of the Master," *The Act of the Mind*, ed. Roy Harvey Pearce and J. Hillis Miller (Baltimore, 1965).

as the fundamental implication of one of his own poems. Of course, this exposition of idea is only part of a proper understanding of a poem by Stevens, but it is an important part in his mind, nevertheless. He underlines the significance of thought to his own poetry by concluding his exegesis with a statement of the function of both emotion and thought in poetry: "The inter-relation between reality and the emotions is the basis of the vitality of literature, between reality and thought, the basis of its power."[4]

This book is written with its major emphasis on the nature and function of idea in the poetry of Stevens and with its major purpose an illumination of the poems. In view of this purpose, readings of a large number of passages from the poems are provided. The over-all plan of the book is expository rather than developmental. Whenever it seems important to uncover hidden or obscure implications, detailed exegesis of a poem is given. With such difficult poetry, paraphrase is often useful to connect passages given detailed study or to reveal an idea submerged in implication.

Throughout the book frequent warnings are given against the assumption of a body of philosophic doctrine in the poetry of Stevens. The intention of this book is not to assign Stevens any position in recent Western thought in spite of the frequent reference to philosophic writings with some themes in common.[5] The concepts of Stevens' poetry, as well as those of the quotations from philosophic writing utilized here, are common to the general body of European thought of the last two centuries. The philosophic passages that are compared to passages of poetry are never considered as possible sources and are quoted only in order to bring out

[4] All the quotations in this paragraph are from *OP*, p. 294.

[5] Stevens belongs to the great tradition of the romantic poets and shares the matrix of thought that underlies their poetry. For a discussion of this subject, see M. H. Abrams, *The Mirror and the Lamp* (New York, 1958), especially Chap. III, "Romantic Analogues of Art and Mind."

the latent concepts of the poetry. The passages were carefully chosen for their specific relevancy of image and idea to a specific poem; an important consideration in the choice of a quotation from a philosophic work was the common imagery of poem and quoted passage. As for the choice of philosophers, most of them are named by Stevens, and the few not mentioned shared the attention of cultivated readers of his period. Whenever possible, citations of philosophic texts refer to the least expensive current edition.

Like any critic of Stevens, I owe a debt of gratitude to the extensive literature devoted to the study of Stevens, especially the excellent work of recent years. This book makes no attempt, however, to survey the field of Stevens criticism.[6] Occasionally in the notes a critical work is cited that is especially appealing to me and pertinent to my own argument.

I owe a large measure of thanks to Professor Aubrey Williams, who gave the manuscript a close reading and made valued suggestions for its final revision. As a result of Miss Barbara Parmelee's careful study of the original manuscript of this book, many improvements have been made in the final version. I wish also to express my gratitude to Mrs. Ann Riddell for her long hours and invaluable assistance in preparing this manuscript for publication.

[6] In general, I am indebted to William Van O'Connor's pioneering study *The Shaping Spirit* (Chicago, 1950) and to the work of Samuel French Morse. I wish to mention also the remarkable insight of Mildred E. Hartsock in several studies of Stevens. She does not expand the glimpses she gives of her understanding of Stevens' images, but all of her essays are of interest to the student of Stevens, especially "Image and Idea in the Poetry of Stevens," *Twentieth Century Literature*, VII (April, 1961), 10–21; and "Wallace Stevens and the 'Rock,'" *Personalist*, XLII (Winter, 1961), 66–76. For a survey of recent studies of Stevens, see Joseph Riddel, "The Contours of Stevens Criticism," *The Act of the Mind*. For a bibliography see Samuel French Morse, Jackson R. Bryer, and Joseph N. Riddel, *Wallace Stevens Checklist and Bibliography of Stevens Criticism* (Denver, 1963). For especially perceptive studies of Stevens' ideas, see the essays of Roy Harvey Pearce and J. Hillis Miller in *The Act of the Mind*.

For their courtesy in granting permission for republication, I wish to thank the editors of the periodicals in which several of these chapters received prior publication. The chapters previously published have received only minor changes and originally appeared as follows: "The Poetry of Thought," with the title "Abstraction and Wallace Stevens," *Criticism* (Winter, 1960); with permission for republication granted by The National Council of Teachers of English, "The Poet of Earth," *College English* (March, 1961); "The River That Flows Nowhere," *The Chicago Review* (November, 1962); and "This Invented World," *ELH* (September, 1961) and again in *The Act of the Mind* (Baltimore, 1965). "Our Nature Is Her Nature" has been accepted for publication in *The American Twenties: Poetry and Prose*, edited by William E. Taylor and Richard E. Langford; at the time this is written, publication is set for January, 1966, by the Everett Edwards Press.

I acknowledge permission granted by Alfred A. Knopf, Incorporated, for use of all quotations from the following copyrighted editions: *The Collected Poems of Wallace Stevens* (1954), *Opus Posthumous* (1957), and *The Necessary Angel* (1951). Permission for use of *Selected Poems by Wallace Stevens*, third printing 1960, was granted by Faber and Faber Limited.

CONTENTS

STEVENS' POETRY OF THOUGHT

I

The Poet of Earth

*... the great poems of heaven and hell have
been written and the great poem of the
earth remains to be written.*[1] Stevens

1

"The planet on the table," Stevens called his book of
poetry. He hoped his poems bore "some feature, some richness, even if only half-perceived," of the reality of earth, "of
the planet of which they were a part." It was the wish of a
poet who found the central concern of his poetry in the
estrangement of the self from a world external to it. Per-
ceiver and thing perceived—this fundamental division of the
mere fact of being and knowing was the basis of poems as
well as conjectures. What certainty could the conscious creature stand upon, considering that its life was lived within the
mind? Where did the rock of reality that was indubitably
there end and the embellishments of the human imagination
begin? Do we know what we know as it is or as we want to
know it? Is vision a looking out or a looking in? Searching
for the boundary where mind ends and world begins, Stevens

[1] *The Necessary Angel* (New York, 1951), p. 142, hereafter cited as *NA*.

continued his lifetime of meditation on the nature of experience up to the date of even the last poems.

Imagination and reality, the blue guitar and things as
they are, middling beast and mystic garden—all these dual-
ities of his—are considerations of one kind or another of this
theme of the mind and the world. The world is the not-self,
that which is reflected on the surface of his consciousness. As
for the mind, it is the conscious self, and Stevens usually
takes this entity to be like a spirit and an indweller bound to
the matter of its body. "You dweller in the dark cabin," he
says, addressing himself to men of imagination, to poets, but
thinking of the dweller as the self inhabiting the darkness of
the body. Thus he opens one of his early poems to earth and
in his amused fashion, characterizing his own gusto for living,
names it "Hymn from a Watermelon Pavilion."

With earth a watermelon pavilion, with the mind as
spirit, as dweller in the dark cabin, whose sense of reality is
obscured as though in a dream but beside whose cabin is
the vivid actual plantain of green reality and the sun:

> And the best cock of red feather
> That crew before the clocks . . . ,

with all the variety of earth, experience for the indwelling
spirit is its happiness. "We stand in the tumult of a festival,"
he says in one of the later poems. In this way the self is
"The Dove in the Belly," to whom "the whole of appearance
is a toy." And yet the self, for all this pleasure in experience,
is still something apart from the physical reality that underlies the nature of appearance.

His usual image of the self is that of a bird, like that of the
sparrow of "Notes toward a Supreme Fiction," with its endless universal cry to the world that surrounds it:

> Bethou me, said sparrow, to the crackled blade,
> And you, and you, bethou me as you blow,
> When in my coppice you behold me be.

Blackbird, peacock, pigeon descending downward to darkness, red robin practicing mere repetitions, crickets "babbling, each one, the uniqueness of its sound"—these are some versions of his idea of the particular existent self. Stevens' final image of individual being is given in one of his last poems, "Of Mere Being," a symbolic portrait of the glory of the animate, of the living creature in its simple existence and as a creature only, the essence of animation conceived even beyond the point at which it is human. The poem represents the ultimate feeling of being, the mere fact of existence itself, the bird as the living self perched in ultimate circumstance, the song, perhaps, its pure activity of being alive:

> The palm at the end of the mind,
> Beyond the last thought, rises
> In the bronze distance,
>
> A gold-feathered bird
> Sings in the palm, without human meaning,
> Without human feeling, a foreign song.

The palm stands at the very end of conception. In the last stanza the wind, a symbol of time perhaps, slowly moves through the branches of the palm that are the ultimate perch of existence. The foreignness, "without human meaning," removes his concept of pure being from the human circumstance into that final realm where the self is a creature only, uttering its life in song that is wordless, and where the bright tropical luxuriance gives a sense of pure and radiant vitality:

> You know then that it is not the reason
> That makes us happy or unhappy.
> The bird sings. Its feathers shine.
>
> The palm stands on the edge of space.
> The wind moves slowly in the branches.
> The bird's fire-fangled feathers dangle down.

By his view of the personal, his presentation of the nature
of self, and by the way in which he regards experience, a
poet puts his invisible signature on meaning. Stevens' concept of being and presentation of experience are given
special qualities and values by his idea of the place of man
in the world, by what is possible to humanity and what is
impossible, by the limitations imposed upon being, by the
necessities of existence. He sharply restricts the possibilities
of being to the earth that holds it and the moment of its life.
Thus, although the self or mind is usually given in this
poetry its archetypal form of psyche or indweller, it is only a
mortal spirit, as in "The Man with the Blue Guitar," XVII,
a poor animal with numbered days, playing the frail guitar
of its poetic imagination:

> . . . The angelic ones
>
> Speak of the soul, the mind. It is
> An animal. The blue guitar—
>
> On that its claws propound, its fangs
> Articulate its desert days.

One necessity of individual being, then, is mortality, and
another is subjectivity, for the mind is a specific of time as
well as a specific of existence or point of identity from which
all the world radiates. These two aspects of being—mortality
and the interdependence of mind and world—engross most
of the discourse of this poetry.

The unique, conceiving, reflecting self of Stevens' poetry
is both container and contained. The world exists only
within the mind, and yet the mind exists only within the
world. An older poet, at least one before Berkeley, would
probably assume that the world of our daily consciousness
is an external world, a common world that each, looking
through transparent eyes, sees to be the same world; only
in the merely fanciful or merely dreamed is there any indi-

vidual version of it. Robert Herrick expressed it this way
(paraphrasing Heraclitus):

> Here we are all, by day; By night w'are hurl'd
> By dreames, each one, into a sevrall world.

For Stevens, however, we are all here by day and by night,
all existing in this reality of which we are part, and yet, at
the same time, it is "a sevrall world" because, as in "The
Sail of Ulysses," it is known by each one only within his own
mind and in terms of his personal realization:

> . . . the world goes round and round
> In the crystal atmospheres of the mind. . . .

In this sense, then, the world is made of the self and the self
of the world. Through the interdependence of personal experience and common experience, through the paradox of
the world as personally conceived and as encompassing all
conceivers, the apparent dualism of Stevens is compounded
into a kind of monism of the inextricable merging of mind
within world and world within mind. These are two things
the poet says in "Extracts from Addresses to the Academy of
Fine Ideas," and yet they cannot be separated, cannot be
told one from another, nor would he wish to distinguish
them:

> . . . He wanted that,
> To face the weather and be unable to tell
> How much of it was light and how much thought. . . .

Stevens is always aware that perception is a complex
psychological occurrence. The real external world unfolds
within our experience of it—and experience is the very life
of the self. Therefore, from the point of view of a self considering that the world he knows exists within his mind and
through his experience of it—from this point of view Stevens,
in "The Sail of Ulysses," presents all the infinite abstraction

of time and space, all of reality, as depending upon the most particular form of being, the "moment of light," the instant of experience in one individual mind:

> The living man in the present place,
> Always, the particular thought
> Among Plantagenet abstractions,
> Always and always, the difficult inch,
> On which the vast arches of space
> Repose, always, the credible thought
> From which the incredible systems spring. . . .[2]

With all this centering of reality upon the self, the moment of a specific experience becomes the only verity, the only available identification for truth, that otherwise mythical abstraction. The truth is "the the," as this poet puts it in "The Man on the Dump," speaking of what he believes while beating on the old tin can, the lard pail of poetry. The specific experience, the *the*, that certain instant of light that is *this* instant, includes the reflective life of the mind as well as the life of the senses. The moment of light, the moment of consciousness, that unfolding event we call experience, including what we think and what we feel as well as what we see, is an infinitely complex realization of self and world. Especially when the conventional illusions are removed, experience "is a visibility of thought, / In which hundreds of eyes in one mind, see at once."

[2] In a passage on the nature of the sublime, Schopenhauer expresses a similar idea in *The World as Will and Idea*, trans. R. B. Haldane and J. Kemp (New York, 1961), pp. 217–18: "He perceives himself, on the one hand, as an individual, as the frail phenomenon of will, which the slightest touch of these forces can utterly destroy, helpless against powerful nature, dependent, the victim of chance, a vanishing nothing in the presence of stupendous might; and on the other hand, as the eternal, peaceful, knowing subject, the condition of the object, and, therefore, the supporter of this whole world; the terrific strife of nature only his idea; the subject itself free and apart from all desires and necessities, in the quiet comprehension of the Ideas." Richard A. Macksey has noted the significance of Schopenhauer for a reader of Stevens in "The Climates of Wallace Stevens," *The Act of the Mind*.

The concluding section of "Esthétique du Mal" is one of many poems Stevens has written that contemplate the inter-action of mind and reality in the present instant of experi-ence. In its first lines Stevens is regarding the physical life that one can live only in the physical present, the actual moment of present circumstance in which we have our being:

> The greatest poverty is not to live
> In a physical world . . . ,

and then, implying that he too is no stranger to ideal worlds, to worlds imagined rather than lived in, wished for rather than known, he continues,

> . . . to feel that one's desire
> Is too difficult to tell from despair. . . .

But whether one's desire is too difficult to express because of despair or too difficult to distinguish from despair cannot be determined here, although the one need not exclude the other. Then the poet, leaping immediately to the idea of the ultimate achievement of desire, that of a pure spiritual life, despairs of such an achievement because of its unreality:

> . . . Perhaps,
> After death, the non-physical people, in paradise,
> Itself non-physical, may, by chance, observe
> The green corn gleaming and experience
> The minor of what we feel. . . .

It seems that for him the physical contains all, even the transcendental, for a completely physical world that does not include the mind and its conception is impossible and incon-ceivable:

> The green corn gleams and the metaphysicals
> Lie sprawling in majors of the August heat,
> The rotund emotions, paradise unknown.

The physical world here is an infinite tissue of mind and matter in which physical material is transformed into non-physical concept and the things conceived and the conception itself are one. In the lines that follow, seeing and hearing seem to stand for all the forms of perception, and what is seen and heard is the infinite complexity of reality, of multiple identities, with each dwelling in his individual world, uniquely conceived and cherished, the eternal changes of time and consciousness flowing through each separate self and yet all of it one world including all and included in each self:

> One might have thought of sight, but who could think
> Of what it sees, for all the ill it sees?
> Speech found the ear, for all the evil sound,
> But the dark italics it could not propound.
> And out of what one sees and hears and out
> Of what one feels, who could have thought to make
> So many selves, so many sensuous worlds,
> As if the air, the mid-day air, was swarming
> With the metaphysical changes that occur,
> Merely in living as and where we live.

Although it may seem that this poem is only a presentation of reality as a complexity of matter and mind, an idea of the real world made up of the minds that conceive it, the selves that feel it, the emotions that color it, as well as the unfelt, devitalized material universe of science, basically it is an expression of wonder and exultation at the existence of life:

> This is the thesis scrivened in delight,
> The reverberating psalm, the right chorale.

Stevens' ardent longing for the physical reality of burgeoning life is a central thesis of his work, and throughout his many years in poetry, from his early days as dweller in the dark cabin crying hail on the watermelon pavilion to the gold-feathered bird singing in the palm at the end of the mind, he celebrates simple vitality. Existence as opposed to

blankness or warmth and affection and consciousness as opposed to black cold and nothingness—these are the opposi-
tions of a poet who finds extinction the only alternative to
"the moment of light," the present and continuous moment
of being. In Stevens' view "the greatest poverty is not to
live / In a physical world" because for him there is no other.
He is not really opposing his reality of the physical present
to something beyond life, to a mystery. The life less than
life—"non-physical people" that he pictures in paradise—is a
fiction without a basis, not even allegory; the "non-physical
people" are presented as though actual; hence, they are straw-
people consumed when tested in the fire of belief. For
Stevens, of course, they only replace a nothingness that he
opposes to the brilliant palpable maze of reality.

2

From this absolute division between consciousness and
blankness come many of the implicit values of Stevens'
poetry—the continual reconsiderations of reality, the vivid
sense of the living moment, the meditations on the nature
of experience. Since there is only the now, even memory and
the past seem unreal and imagined, almost. "It is an illusion
that we were ever alive," he says in "The Rock." A life
remembered is a fantastic thing, with its changing desires and
continual defeats of human intention—defeats engendered
in the very nature of existence, with love and warmth and
happiness subject to the cancellation of the flux:

> The meeting at noon at the edge of the field seems like
>
> An invention, an embrace between one desperate clod
> And another in a fantastic consciousness,
> In a queer assertion of humanity. . . .

Thus, with all reality held in the living instant of experience, the past is only a "Vacancy in the Park," an emptiness of March, where the snow that bears wandering footprints, the traces of aimless happenings, will soon melt:

> March . . . Someone has walked across the snow,
> Someone looking for he knows not what.

With the past no longer a reality and extinction at the end of the future, existence in itself is almost an impossibility, something intrinsically difficult, a kind of bravery. And yet, the present moment of one's life is all that can be truly conceived and all that one truly has.

Since nothingness is too absolute for realization, Stevens considers in one poem, "The Well Dressed Man with a Beard," the fact that the mind cannot rest in the idea of any final negation and must seek for something to remain— although all the past, all the rejected things "slide over the western cataract"—something to stay, upon which a future would depend, even if only "a speech / Of the self that must sustain itself on speech." Life must depend on believing in that one infallible thing. Then, holding in imagination, his ear over the sleeping form of the self, like one listening to life within a hive, he knows that the mind can never be satisfied to resign itself to nothingness:

> Green in the body, out of a petty phrase,
> Out of a thing believed, a thing affirmed:
> The form on the pillow humming while one sleeps,
> The aureole above the humming house . . .
>
> It can never be satisfied, the mind, never.

It is true that Stevens considers death to be a condition of existence, but point of view is of vital importance here, and such an idea of death can be presented only from the point of view of one who is existing. He can say from the vantage of existence that the images his poems hold of death "make

certain how being / Includes death and the imagination."
This brings to mind our usual way of regarding nothingness,
for when we speak of nothingness, we unconsciously consider
it as though it were a kind of somethingness. Stevens refuses
to project his imagination into death and consider it a kind
of life.

"The Owl in the Sarcophagus," one of Stevens' longer and
later poems, is a meditation not on death but on the idea of
death, and in his meditation he is able to conceive of extinction only by personifying sleep and peace, the usual self-
comforting concepts of death without resurrection. The sus-
taining quality of this finely modulated elegy is its gentle
compassionate tone mingled with its steady advertence to
annihilation. That moment "on the edges of oblivion" when
the energy of being is no more than a retinal image after
the light is out, the very instant of death—this is the farthest
he can go in conception: "O exhalation, O fling without a
sleeve." Of his personifications of memory and sleep and
peace, he says, "This is the mythology of modern death."
Realizing that the self cannot conceive of its own absolute
destruction, he knows that what he is personifying is only a
means the mind has of imagining the retention of itself as
an entity even after death. Thus, we create forms for an
identity in death (like that of eternal sleep) just as we create
forms for our identity in life:

> It is a child that sings itself to sleep,
> The mind, among the creatures that it makes,
> The people, those by which it lives and dies.

Here Stevens indicates a major postulate of so many of his
poems—his thesis that the mind creates forms and personifications, that it humanizes reality in order that it may live on
its own terms. The mind's creatures are not only the self
that it conceives itself to be but also conceptions of other

people and abstract persons, too, like the common man, the
soldier, poets, statesmen, heroes, deities.

In this regard man is the artificer of the circumstances of
his own life. Stevens goes as far as Protagoras ("Man is the
measure of all things") in his essays, as in this statement from
The Necessary Angel: "The greatest truth we could hope to
discover, in whatever field we discovered it, is that man's
truth is the final resolution of everything."[3] Man's own
existence, composed by himself in the specific terms of his
conceptions, "is the heroic subject of all study."[4] Heaven
and hell and, in a sense, earth, too, are imagined places of
this existence, but Stevens himself refuses to enter into a
conception of that which is apart from one's own immediate
experience. Beyond earth he will not project himself. Thus,
his agnosticism is a position he assumes as a result of this
refusal and of his conviction that a conception of a non-
human sphere is a humanizing of something only imagined.
"It comes to this," he says, summarizing his position in the
posthumous essay "Two or Three Ideas," "that we use the
same faculties when we write poetry that we use when we
create gods or when we fix the bearing of men in reality."[5]

But he is willing to contemplate the human sphere from
the point of view of the objective observer and see man
encompassed by that which cannot be conceived. One of
Stevens' finest later poems, "The Auroras of Autumn," II,
presents the condition of man with just such a possible external unknown impinging on that condition. The image
used is that of a man walking on the shore, facing the approaching winter, feeling the cold of the north wind, aware
of the mystery of the aurora borealis above him. The image
reminds one of Donne's fear "that when I have spunne / My

[3] P. 175.
[4] *Ibid.*, p. 176.
[5] *OP*, p. 216.

last thread, I shall perish on the shore." In Stevens, no personal fate seems involved, and much of the poignancy of this poem is conveyed by its neutral tone, its subdued effects, its presentation of dramatic material through a simple depiction. This masterpiece of modulation gives a general perspective of Stevens' vision of the human circumstance:

> Farewell to an idea . . . A cabin stands,
> Deserted, on a beach. It is white,
> As by a custom or according to
>
> An ancestral theme or as a consequence
> Of an infinite course. The flowers against the wall
> Are white, a little dried, a kind of mark
>
> Reminding, trying to remind, of a white
> That was different, something else, last year
> Or before, not the white of an aging afternoon,
>
> Whether fresher or duller, whether of winter cloud
> Or of winter sky, from horizon to horizon.
> The wind is blowing the sand across the floor.
>
> Here, being visible is being white,
> Is being of the solid of white, the accomplishment
> Of an extremist in an exercise . . .
>
> The season changes. A cold wind chills the beach.
> The long lines of it grow longer, emptier,
> A darkness gathers though it does not fall
>
> And the whiteness grows less vivid on the wall.
> The man who is walking turns blankly on the sand.
> He observes how the north is always enlarging the
>   change,
>
> With its frigid brilliances, its blue-red sweeps
> And gusts of great enkindlings, its polar green,
> The color of ice and fire and solitude.

The import of this poem depends upon the significance of its bare images—the deserted cabin on the winter beach,

the blowing sand, the dried flowers, the clouded sky, the
man alone on the sand, the aurora borealis, and the abstractions of darkness and coldness and whiteness.

"Farewell to an idea," the poem opens. It is the first of
three *adieux* of "The Auroras of Autumn," Stevens' sequence
of ten meditations on the human condition encompassed by
the unknowable. The "idea" of this farewell, in accordance
with the terms of the rest of the poem, can be assumed to be
an idea of individual being. With "here, being visible is
being white," an identification of whiteness with the existent
is made. To be white is to exist. Living, being actual, "is
being of the solid of white." To live on is, in his ironic com-
ment, "the accomplishment / Of an extremist in an exer-
cise," for this is a poem of one who has existed on into the
winter of his life. The only color in the poem occurs in the
aurora, "the color of ice and fire and solitude," and stands
for that which is beyond existence.

The sand blowing across the floor seems to be a time
symbol derived from the movement of sand in an hour glass.
The darkness that "gathers though it does not fall" suggests
the imminence of death, and the cold wind chilling the beach
implies a relationship between the flowing of time and this
imminence.

The season changes. Existence, the whiteness of the wall,
is fading. The beach that the wind chills, the lines of which
"grow longer, emptier," where the man turns blankly, refers
to the course of an existence. The man observes, like one
who watches the inevitable, that the North with its lights is
always increasing the cold, enlarging the change of the season
of life. These lights are the aurora with its "frigid brilliances,"
an image of vast and inscrutable forces.

Stevens mitigates the severity of this depiction somewhat in
another poem. In "The Auroras of Autumn," VIII, the
aurora borealis, the lights that are not human lights, are not
a dark untoward expression of some unknown malice. They

are a natural event and part of the essential innocence; human existence, the life of the mind that is an awakening, a consciousness in the midst of the unconscious, is encompassed by the innocence of earth—innocent because spontaneous and childlike or without purpose or intent:

> So, then, these lights are not a spell of light,
> A saying out of a cloud, but innocence.
> An innocence of the earth and no false sign
>
> Or symbol of malice. That we partake thereof,
> Lie down like children in this holiness,
> As if, awake, we lay in the quiet of sleep. . . .

The innocence that he affirms in this passage is no more than a projection of his austere and candid agnosticism. In fact, his whole view of the human circumstance is severe in its restriction to the little that it will allow for confidence, almost no more than the space he occupies and the time of his insight of the present moment—these and his boundless imagination that holds all within its "crystal atmosphere," including the imminence of its own mortality. But this restricted view that could well find the bitter utterance of despair is expressed with a courage and a balanced humor that are part of the rare and individual quality of this poetry. These virtues are apparent in "Things of August," VII, in which the poet climbs down from his perspective of his own whole view of man, down from his tower to "the nature of his chair," to the familiar details of his concept of self. Sitting securely in that moment of his life, he considers with the serenity and the satisfaction of an achieved vision "the spun sky and the high and deadly view" from which he has descended:

> It was curious to have to descend
> And, seated in the nature of his chair,
> To feel the satisfactions
> Of that transparent air.

II

Our Nature Is Her Nature

*A naturalistic conception of things is a
great work of imagination,—greater, I
think, than any dramatic or moral mythology: it is a conception fit to inspire great
poetry, and in the end, perhaps, it will
prove the only conception able to inspire
it.*[1] Santayana

1

At the time of his first book, Stevens had already conceived
for his poetry a minimum basis of thought or, if not thought,
at least a consistent view of things. In *Harmonium* he expresses a rudimentary naturalism that is usually little more
than a sense of the reality of things about him—things moving
and changing in the flux of time and experience. Its basis
is an inherent skepticism that rejects the transcendent and
can never rest in any explanation or circumscription of the
world. Limiting the scope of his confidence to the immediate,

[1] *Three Philosophical Poets* (Garden City, n.d.), p. 27. Although the
naturalistic view is predominant in the poetry of Stevens, some few de-
partures from this viewpoint can be found, for instance, "Notes toward
a Supreme Fiction," the fifth stanza of Poem IV of the first section.

he conjectures an indefinite and unknowable expanse beyond the impression of the moment.

To hold that the world is an indeterminable presence is to reject the idea of the microcosm. Stevens is too much of a skeptic to feel that he can gain the whole through a part, that like Blake he can see the world in a grain of sand. "The Indigo Glass in the Grass" explicitly states that in no object nor conjunction of objects can the world be contained, and in "The Comedian as the Letter C" the poet doubts that the world can be comprehended in one man's vision of it or even in any conjunction of human points of view:

> What is one man among so many men?
> What are so many men in such a world?

In an illimitable and incomprehensible world of continual flux, the human element is only one among many elements. The unity of the world as composed by one mind is only the unity of one life lived, and even that, like Crispin's, involves a continual readjustment of the sense of the world; for as the poet asks in extenuation of these readjustments, these vicissitudes of anyone's idea of the world:

> Can one man think one thing and think it long?
> Can one man be one thing and be it long?

The unspoken reply is the obvious negative. Crispin's or anyone's next moment will differ from the last and most probably resemble it as well.

Resemblances and differences are significant elements in experience for Stevens. They structure the natural world for him and are constituents of his naturalistic emphasis on the appearance of things in poems like "Sea Surface Full of Clouds" or "The Load of Sugar-Cane."[2] Some years later than *Harmonium* he wrote "Three Academic Pieces,"[3] the

[2] For a more elaborate discussion of the idea of resemblances in Stevens, see Robert Pack, *Wallace Stevens* (New Brunswick, 1958), Chap. 3.

[3] See *NA*, pp. 71–82, for the quotations from this essay.

opening essay of which is a brief account of the unity that
resemblance gives to one's sense of the world. Simple resemblance itself is considered here to be "one of the significant components of the structure of reality." Resemblance
of one thing to another is part of the continuity of experience. "It binds together. It is the base of appearance," the
essay explains. Several poems in *Harmonium* anticipate the
idea discussed in his essay—the idea of the unity that resemblance gives to the content of experience. In "Domination of Black," for instance, resemblance binds together
everything named and is the significant component of the
sense of reality of the poem. The colors of the bushes and
of the leaves recur in the color of fire; the movement of the
leaves in the wind is repeated in the turning of shadows and
flames; and the color and movement of the leaves suggest
peacocks' tails:

> The colors of their tails
> Were like the leaves themselves
> Turning in the wind. . . .

The pivot of all these resemblances is the image of the
movement of things in wind, and wind brings to mind the
idea of the flux of time. By the same process of connotation,
peacock symbolizes mind or self (at least for the speaker of
the poem) with all its color turning in the flux and its cry
against mortality. Connotation itself is created by the activity
of a mind tracing resemblances. "Perhaps the whole field of
connotation is based on resemblance," the essay conjectures.
In the poem connotations for the idea of mortality shared by
hemlock, shadow, and night are emphasized by resemblance,
for all these things share a symbolic darkness. Stevens' essay
says of this enhancement of a shared element or quality: "If
resemblance is described as a partial similarity between two
dissimilar things, it complements and reinforces that which
the two dissimilar things have in common."

Resemblance is a thread of continuity from one impression to another followed by the mind seeking relations among things. Stevens probably was familiar with the chapter on "The One and the Many" in William James' *Pragmatism* and the discussion there of the various kinds of lines of continuity that bind the world together. James indicates the necessity of a sense of the continuity of things on the field of consciousness, notes that the mind can pass in many ways from one thing to another, speaks of the lines of influence or relationship that can be traced: "Following any such line you pass from one thing to another till you may have covered a good part of the universe's extent."[4] He says that to follow simple continuity, it is even enough to move from one thing to another and say that there is this and this and this.

Tracing the structure of reality through the discernment of resemblance or of any other lines of continuity that bind the world together, the mind is engaged in its natural activity and becomes the "secretive hunter" of "Stars at Tallapoosa":

> Let these be your delight, secretive hunter,
> Wading the sea-lines, moist and ever-mingling,
> Mounting the earth-lines, long and lax, lethargic.
> These lines are swift and fall without diverging.

The swift lines falling without divergence and the lines between the stars of the first stanza are all lines of relationship and cognitive interconnection, as even the imaginary lines of starlight must be. All these lines are part of the continuity of experience and compose what William James describes as "innumerable kinds of connection that special things have with other special things."[5] The poet finds that this tracing of relations and interconnections is like the interior life of feeling and association:

[4] New York, 1955, p. 93.
[5] *Ibid.*

> . . . But in yourself is like:
> A sheaf of brilliant arrows flying straight,
> Flying and falling straightway for their pleasure. . . .

Then the poet reconsiders and discards the old figure of the arrows of thought to describe the successive impulses of immediate experience. The quick activity of memory is a closer parallel with its "nimblest motions," as the poet beautifully describes the instant and straightway recoveries of the fervor of past experience hidden in the darkness of possible remembrance:

> Or, if not arrows, then the nimblest motions,
> Making recoveries of young nakedness
> And the lost vehemence the midnights hold.[6]

---

[6] In no sense a source, Santayana's *Realms of Being* (New York, 1942) has several images that parallel and illuminate Stevens' poem. For the darkness of the lines between the stars in Stevens' poem ("The lines are much too dark and much too sharp"), Santayana has this parallel concept of light: "It traverses space unceasingly in a thousand directions, leaving it perfectly black and cold" (p. 237). For Stevens' "sheaf of brilliant arrows"—arrows that are "in yourself"—there is this passage of Santayana that relates Apollo's arrows to the inner light of intuition: "To call this cosmic agency light is a poetic metaphor, as if we called it Phoebus; which indeed we might do without absurdity, since Apollo besides his golden locks had his invisible arrows; and these were the dread reality of the god. Only the obvious essence of brightness shining in intuition is light proper" (p. 237). For Stevens' line "The body is no body to be seen," there is Santayana's parallel concept: "Sometimes, as in deep thought, no image of one's own body figures at all in intuition" (p. 246). For the idea of continuity in Stevens' poem—the earth-lines, the sea-lines— there is Santayana's image of "the substantial thread" connecting phenomena: "Action cannot accept phenomena simply as phenomena, but must trace the substantial thread on which they are strung together" (p. 220). Santayana speaks also of "a thin thread of calculable continuity that runs through immediate experience" (p. 226). For Stevens' "secretive hunter" there is Santayana's characterization of the self as a hunter of the real in this passage (the chase here is Santayana's figurative expression for all physical experience): "The hunter and the hunted believe in something ambushed and imminent: present images are little to them but signs for coming events" (p. 201).

2

The mind, the secretive hunter that seeks within itself the various forms of relationship, imposes the unity of its own being upon all of its experiences. As Stevens goes on to explain in "Three Academic Pieces," a spontaneous mythology results when the mind projects the human image outward and interprets the world anthropomorphically. Like Narcissus discovering himself in the mirror of the pool, the human self sees his humanity reflected in the world around him: "he sought out his image everywhere because it was the principle of his nature to do so." The image seen may be no more than a formulation of a feeling of simple pleasure in normal experience; it may seem to be a discovery of the appealing nature of the scene although only an echo of inner health and wakefulness.

Personification is the verbal form of this spontaneous mythology. Stevens' own use of myth usually goes no further than a basic central image that embodies a complex of feeling and desire related by metaphor to the natural world. In "The Paltry Nude Starts on a Spring Voyage," there is the first bare showing of the season, a few weeds seen in thin sunlight, and, above them, the symbolic figure of the early year, the paltry nude starting on the spring voyage that would assuredly transform her into summer's goldener image of spontaneous desire. Spring is the time of year associated with the archetypal image of bareness and immaturity, the Kore or maiden, and the poet remembers her even in the midst of summer as a time "when radiance came running down, slim through the bareness." Long awaited before it comes, its weather and its essence are desired like the desired image of woman. "Depression before Spring" expresses this desire in the figure of one expected in "slipper green"—in the verdure of the season. It is one of Stevens' many adaptations of the archetypal image of woman projected as a personification upon the world of one's impressions.

The crow of the cock in "Depression before Spring" carries an echo of the idea of the procreative urge, for the cock elsewhere in *Harmonium* represents the primal creative element by a phallic pun that recurs as "damned universal cock" in "Bantams in Pine-Woods" and as "the perfect cock" of "The Bird with the Coppery, Keen Claws." Finding in the desire of male for female an analogy to the desire of life for springtime, in "Depression before Spring" the poet sets up a series based on the analogy: cock for hen, man for woman, poet for springtime personified as woman. Male calls, cock crows, but no hen answers:

> But ki-ki-ri-ki
> Brings no rou-cou,
> No rou-cou-cou.

The male "Ho! Ho!" and even the poem itself, which seems to be a poet's invocation of the longed-for season, brings no apparition of the first green answer to desire:

> But no queen comes
> In slipper green.

"The divine ingénue" of "Last Looks at the Lilacs" is also a personification of reality manifested in the essence of a season. Her indifference to what it is that embraces her innocence is consistent with the usual indifference of nature to man in Stevens' work, and her innocence is that of the undirected accidental course of reality. Personified as one having the innocence that is an ignorance and an absence of any ill intention, Nature does not care who "marries her innocence thus, / So that her nakedness is near."

Her companion, the analytical but unintuitive caliper, is man in his practical, unimaginative relationship with earth; he is a boorish instrument of measurement who has lost the mythic vision of things and is no longer able to sense the primal heat of the season of procreation, the Floréal or month of flowering. Practical, reasonable man is adjured to take his last look at the lilacs, whose lavender bloom displays the proliferation of things in nature; for seeing this flowering as no more than meaningless detail, as trash, he cannot see it as the outward manifestation of the vital principle ˙of natural growth, and no longer feels

> Her body quivering in the Floréal
>
> Toward the cool night and its fantastic star,
> Prime paramour and belted paragon,
> Well-booted, rugged, arrogantly male. . . .

Union with the male principle, "patron and imager of the gold Don John," is a metaphoric account of the fruition of the year—the springtime earth suffused in the warmth and light that transform it into the earth of summer.

"O Florida, Venereal Soil" uses a kindred body of personification. Addressed to the archetypal woman as earth image— here identified with the actual place, the soil of Florida— the poem beseeches her to reduce the meaningless variety of disparate objects that distract the consciousness and asks her to conceal herself in darkness and quietude. After the dreadful sundry of miscellaneous reality and the confusions of daylight, the mind is tormented even at night by the ferment of undirected feeling. What the poet seeks instead is the calm of the night sea and sky with its simple composition of cloud and stars:

> Donna, donna, dark,
> Stooping in indigo gown
> And cloudy constellations. . . .

Invoking the vision of myth, the poet asks of the symbolic figure of earth that she reveal to the lover of reality, to the consciousness, no more than the few specific things that the

mind can attend when it gives something significance or
regards something for its own sake. "Conceal yourself," the
poem entreats, or if you manifest yourself in the darkness,
disclose through the mythical vision

> Fewest things to the lover—
> A hand that bears a thick-leaved fruit,
> A pungent bloom against your shade.

These are significatory images for the consciousness that is
the lover of reality—an image of creativeness (the hand
symbol) holding an emblem of fruition, or a perfection, some
ideal form emerging out of creative darkness.

3

Male and female principles in the poetry of Stevens are
often representations of consciousness as male lover and of
reality as anonymous woman—unknown because reality can
never be realized objectively. "Le Monocle de Mon Oncle,"
however, presents the male-female relationship as simply
what it is, for this poem is a discourse by man to woman on
love looked at through the monocle, the point of view of
middle age. In the opening poem the poet, from the vantage
of his years, addresses the beloved, mocking her as the mythical goddess of love. He deprecates her powers, for he has
come to the time of life when love is not all. Now there is
nothing that can overwhelm him like the magnificence of
poetry and its sharp verbal paradoxes:

> There is not nothing, no, no, never nothing,
> Like the clashed edges of two words that kill.

The poem clashes its negatives against each other with a
display of the combat of words and their cancelings. Then
the poet remembers his beloved in the time of youthful love,

and from deep within him sorrow for what love once was rises into expression as from a well of tears:

> . . . And then
> A deep up-pouring from some saltier well
> Within me, bursts its watery syllable.

The naturalistic significance of the poem, its major theme, is revealed in the poet's recognition that the course of love is only the course of nature. There is first the common ground of human experience: "Shall I uncrumple this much-crumpled thing," this common theme of love, the poet asks, and in the eighth stanza he finds love to be a cycle, the stages of which are repeated for each individual:

> An ancient aspect touching a new mind.
> It comes, it blooms, it bears its fruit and dies.

And they, the poet and his beloved, have come to that time in the course of love (and its course is only an aspect of the course of nature) when they are overripe fruit of a tree. The tree he has in mind has a certain tip, he says, indicating by the phallic image the fact that the sexual nature of love remains while the individual passions that visit it come and go:

> It stands gigantic, with a certain tip
> To which all birds come sometime in their time.
> But when they go that tip still tips the tree.

The law of sexual motivation is not the sole factor, the poet maintains in the eleventh stanza, for choice of one by another is selective and passionate. The stanza concludes with an image that illustrates the ambivalent nature of love—its primal organic basis and its shared imaginative quality. Lover and beloved sit beside the pool of pink, "clippered with lilies scudding the bright chromes," depicting the conceptual nature of their affections, while a frog "boomed from his very belly odious chords." The image of the frog is one of many that set forth as the major theme of the poem the idea that love, with all its imaginative and affective involvement, is a natural event emanating from an organic source.

4

In "Le Monocle de Mon Oncle" the course of love is no more than the course of nature, and in "The Comedian as the Letter C," the course of thought is only the natural course of a man's life. Crispin, like any man, must live by synecdoche and conceive, in terms of the small part known, the indefinite unknown. Reconstituting his philosophy, his idea of the nature of the world, over and over, Crispin composes each time out of his minuscule point of view and out of his vagrant subjectivity what he trusts at the moment is a true and permanent conception of reality, as valid for the next altered moment as for the present.

To illustrate the fact that the human idea of the world is a continual revision, Crispin's life is traced in terms of shifting perspectives of reality. From sea to tropics and then to North America, from introspective sea voyager to settler in Carolina and father of four—these changes of place and role are also changes of mind. Crispin's continual effort to adjust his philosophy to reality is only a form of adaptation to place and condition. During his voyage he loses the beliefs of his homeland and sees himself as diminished in the midst of ocean. Confronted by the blankness of matter during his ocean voyage, Crispin assumes that now he is able to see the veritable thing in itself. He looks at vast sea and endless sky and asks what it is that all this mystery of appearance could be since apparently it has no source in anything as human as a deity, for all the pretences and stratagems of the human ego are lost in the blankness of the non-human.

Crispin seeks to intuit the reality of things, wishes to realize them as he trusts they may be in their own objective existence. Just as the later poet of "An Ordinary Evening in New Haven" sought "nothing beyond reality," the younger poet of *Harmonium* refused to look beyond reality because he believed there was nothing beyond it. In a naturalistic conception, the sole ground of an existence is its reality. To be real is almost a quality in itself for reality is the truth of existence, a feeling of the verity of things. Since a trust in the reality of things and selves fills out the void that would otherwise exist without a belief in a transcendent ground of being, the word *reality* holds an unconscious store of feeling in Stevens' use of it.

Even the self becomes a configuration and essence of surrounding reality in a naturalistic poem; therefore, it is fitting that Crispin considers man to be only a product of the complex of what is specific for a certain place and time. This is a conclusion offered in "Anecdote of Men by the Thousand," with its statement that the self is formed by its perceptions:

> The soul, he said, is composed
> Of the external world.

The poet of "Theory" in like manner accepts David Hume's notion that the self is composed of the floating empirical moment and flatly asserts, "I am what is around me." Similarly Crispin concludes that "his soil is man's intelligence," and this remark holds many of the implications of the assertion, many years later in "Things of August," that "the world images for the beholder" and the self is "the possessed of sense not the possessor." All of these assumptions about the nature of the self make it a natural part of a natural world.

At the end of "The Comedian as the Letter C," Crispin is the realist for whom "what is is what should be." He discovers that the good of experience emerges from the fecundity of the natural world and that its events include him and its forces impel him. If the ordinary round, composed of daily joys and evenings that disclose the infinity of night, if the succession of days "saps" any man, as it does Crispin, it is not that it diminishes or draws away his hopes and ambitions but that the quotidian "saps" as the sun does, draining away each day and giving another.

Crispin's last deduction is that the world, simple and familiar as a turnip, is the same unknowable but ponderable reality, for as a totality the world is only an imagined thing. At the same time, it is the true substance of experience. Hence, it is "its ancient purple," according to Stevens' blue-red color symbolism[7] (blue for the imagined and red for the real), the imagined-real colors merging into purple; for the world, in itself the essence of the real, is only a conception carried wherever man goes and reproduced in each generation. It is always the same incomprehensible whole, "the same insoluble lump"; and the fatalist who believes that what is, is what must be

> Stepped in and dropped the chuckling down his craw,
> Without grace or grumble. . . .

To swallow the realization that the world is unknowable is a simple and spontaneous act for the naturalist who assumes that man and his works are a part of the natural order and do not transcend it.

The poet concludes that all of Crispin's philosophizing, all his attempts at

> Illuminating, from a fancy gorged
> By apparition, plain and common things,

---

[7] For a general study of this subject, see George McFadden, "Probings for an Integration: Color Symbolism in Wallace Stevens," *MP* (February, 1961). Santayana uses the color purple to designate a subjective version of the real. Speaking of the subjective bent of thinking that sees the universe from a moral and religious point of view, he says, "But this strain of subjectivity is not in all respects an evil; it is a warm purple dye." *Character and Opinion in the United States* (New York, 1956), p. 20.

> Sequestering the fluster from the year,
> Making gulped potions from obstreperous drops,

are a natural effort to comprehend the nature of reality in the
midst of the confusion of the flux of feeling and thought and
changing appearance—an attempt to understand a whole
from a part and to see the world in an impression. Crispin's
philosophizing is a natural response of the conceiving creature. Like Santayana, the poet realizes that "thought is a
form of life, and should be conceived on the analogy of nu-
trition, generation, and art."[8] Although Crispin has proved
nothing by all of his speculation, his shifting philosophy is
the natural course of one man's mind, and his life is only
another incident in the course of human life:

> . . . what can all this matter since
> The relation comes, benignly, to its end?
>
> So may the relation of each man be clipped.

The end is benign because the course of Crispin's life is the
course of nature. Crispin's vain attempt to understand a
world from the small vantage of an impression, confused and
muddled by the subjectivity and irrational reflection of selfhood, is only the tale or relation of each man. It is an expression of the human nature that is only a part of the larger
nature of things and events. And so, the poet concludes
ambiguously, may the account of each man be ended; or (as
the alternate meaning) the account of each man may be
ended thus.

5

According to the narration of Crispin's peripatetic speculation in "The Comedian as the Letter C" and the explanation
of the organic nature of love in "Le Monocle de Mon Oncle,"

[8] *The Life of Reason* (New York, 1962), I, 54.

thought and affection are conceived to be parts of the natural world. In "Sunday Morning" Stevens places the whole man in the natural order, and in the skeptical tradition of naturalism, he draws a parallel between the indigenous life of man and that of the wild creatures: man is a natural creature like the deer and the quail and has his cycle of maturity like the wild berries. His descent to death is represented symbolically by the descent of pigeons to darkness at evening, sinking downward with "ambiguous undulations." The world that man inhabits is the chaos of chance and the accidental being of naturalism; he is isolated from all moments other than his own by the inescapable separations of expanses of time:

> We live in an old chaos of the sun,
> Or old dependency of day and night,
> Or island solitude, unsponsored, free,
> Of that wide water, inescapable.

Since for Stevens nothing is truly credible except present being, happiness occurs only in immediate experience. The earth itself offers man his only possible paradise because it is the only possible location for his existence. Therefore, the proper subject of the poet who is also a naturalist is his individual sense of the world. This is a continuing conviction of Stevens, and many years after *Harmonium* he observes in "A Collect of Philosophy" that the poet's world is his constant subject: "the poet's world is intended to be a world, which yet remains to be celebrated and which, at bottom, the poets probably hope will always remain to be celebrated."[9] In the same essay he says that the poet's world is his native sphere, the sphere that he has made his own by the individual version of it that he conceives: "The poet's native sphere is the sphere of which du Bellay wrote: 'my village . . . my own small

[9] For the three quotations from this essay, see *OP,* pp. 198–99.

house.' " When Stevens adds that "the poet's world is this present world plus imagination," he means that the poet's world is the world that he knows and continually realizes in the many variations of his own individual conception of it. Thus, the poet's world is the same world that any man finds in his vivid actual apprehension of it, that he finds

> . . . in comforts of the sun,
> In pungent fruit and bright, green wings, or else
> In any balm or beauty of the earth. . . .

In the infinite complexity of multiple experience, the world, by its occasions, continually opens out for the endless celebration of poetry or the endless enrichment of the self. In the seventh stanza of "Sunday Morning," the symbolic image of the ring of men chanting their celebration of the paradise of present being and "their boisterous devotion to the sun" represents the celebration of poetry and the enjoyment of sensibility. By their devotion to the sun, they address themselves to both a symbol and an instance of the objective reality about them—objective only as a source because existing in the inner conceptual life of organic being. Their chant arising "out of their blood returning to the sky" is addressed to the non-human or savage source of experience and they address it

> Not as a god, but as a god might be,
> Naked among them, like a savage source.

In this early presentation of the sun symbolism that recurs in all the successive volumes of Stevens' poetry, the basic elements are present. The reality for which the sun stands is, as a savage source, a primal base from which the elaborations of an individual understanding of it may arise. It is naked in the special sense that Stevens has for the word—naked in that it is unconscious and is a presence in itself before it is clothed by conception. Santayana uses the word in this sense in the long philosophical metaphor from *Scepticism and Animal Faith*,[10] in which ideas are clothes and things are bodies. Reality is bare of conscious thought, or as Santayana says,

> All nature runs about naked, and quite happy; and I am not so remote from nature as not to revert on occasion to that nakedness—which is unconsciousness—with profound relief.

The chant of the ring of men is a poem to the reality of existence and a hymn of faith that men themselves are only a manifestation of the natural world and part of the infinite variety of the natural order. The dew upon their feet, from the grasses of that earth from which they come and to which they will return, symbolizes the likeness of man to the natural growth of the fields:

> And whence they came and whither they shall go
> The dew upon their feet shall manifest.

As to this origin and destination, "Anatomy of Monotony," a poem that substantiates the naturalism of "Sunday Morning," is even more explicit. Earth, the mother, and all her creatures share, the poem implies, the same nature and the same fate. Man emerged from the creative energy of an earth lewder or more procreant in its creative phase than now. Whatever he may be, his nature can never transcend hers:

> If from the earth we came, it was an earth
> That bore us as a part of all the things
> It breeds and that was lewder than it is.
> Our nature is her nature. . . .

Stevens' naturalism is immediately apparent in the basic mythic vision of nature as woman, whether mother or be-

---

[10] New York, 1955, p. 72. *Scepticism and Animal Faith* and *Harmonium* appeared in the same year (1923).

loved. The apparent duality of mind and world that permeates his poetry may seem, in a superficial view, to be at variance with a naturalistic conception of things, but mind in Stevens, as in Schopenhauer or Santayana, is only nature looking at itself. If the world exists as it is only in a particular experience of it, if the world that we know is a conceived world, the one who conceives is only a part of that world. His nature is her nature, or, to state the figure in an abstraction, the subject is part of the object.

III

Variations on a Nude

When, therefore, in dreams and other spontaneous products, we meet with an unknown female figure whose significance oscillates between the extremes of goddess and whore, it is advisable to let her keep her independence and not reduce her arbitrarily to something known.[1] Jung

1

A common notion of our century holds that poetry, meditation, in fact all verbal reflection may be regarded as essentially a discourse: there is the voice of a poem or of a thought, and as a secondary person there is the anonymous ear, the possible auditor—perhaps no more than the tacit presence of a receiving mind that the occasion of any utterance implies. The auditor may or may not be named or imagined. Stevens, for instance, named Swenson, ephebe, serpent, woolen massa. Even when named, the one addressed, it can be assumed, is another self rather than another person, even rather than

[1] C. G. Jung and C. Kerényi, *Essays on a Science of Mythology*, trans. R. F. C. Hull (New York, 1963), p. 173.

the reader, and the poem itself may be considered a formal embodiment of what is assumed to be an interior discourse.

In many poems Stevens addresses a hypothetical self in the inner world or inner room of consciousness: "In the central of our being." When he speaks of the mind, it seems that he speaks of another self, as in this notation from the "Adagia": "It is necessary to propose an enigma to the mind. The mind always proposes a solution." Another maxim from the "Adagia" is more explicit: "When the mind is like a hall in which thought is like a voice speaking, the voice is always that of someone else."[2] Whether the subjective element is listening or speaking, there is an implication of inner discourse of a self with a projected other self. Santayana describes the interior converse of the intelligence as discourse with an unseen auditor: "and intelligence talks and talks to an interlocutor—the mind of another man or god or an eventual self of one's own. . . ."[3]

An image of the self objectified and seen as though looked upon from above occurs in many guises in the work of Stevens. There is the form on the pillow of "The Well Dressed Man with a Beard," the humming or living self. This is the objectified image of the self known subliminally as still alive and present even during the blank of sleep. Bergson, in

[2] Both quotations from the "Adagia" are in *OP*, p. 168. These aphorisms were quoted in one of the basic documents on Stevens, Louis L. Martz, "Wallace Stevens: The World as Meditation," *Wallace Stevens*, ed. Marie Borroff (Englewood, 1963). This illuminating study discusses the discourse of a poem of Stevens as a natural secular meditation offering some parallels to the formal procedure of devotional meditation. My own discussion of the idea of discourse in a poem of Stevens has the quite different purpose of indicating the imagined speaker and auditor in a poem in order to describe the projection out of the self of an image that is an embodiment of feeling. I hope that this introduction will cast some light on the significance of Stevens' archetypal woman as reality. My own brief presentation of Stevens' incipient myth emerging from inner discourse leans on Ernst Cassirer, *Language and Myth*, trans. Susanne K. Langer (New York, 1946), pp. 17–38 and 62–85.

[3] *Scepticism*, p. 283.

a passage from *Creative Evolution* that uses this image of self-awareness during sleep, suggests that the subjective self cannot conceive of a void or absence of self. Self-awareness is a necessity of consciousness, and as Bergson maintains, we are always accompanied by a sense of the self existing in some context of introspection or as a presence in the world: "I may suppose that I sleep without dreaming or that I have ceased to exist; but at the very instant when I make this supposition, I conceive myself, I imagine myself watching over my slumber or surviving my annihilation, and I give up perceiving myself from within only by taking refuge in the perception of myself from without."[4]

Bergson's account of self as a reality continuing while the reflective self is asleep implies a self that is pure subjectivity and also a self that is an object with the same kind of reality that all the other content of experience has. A further development of this division of a life is made by Stevens in "The Men That are Falling," and here the conceiver or the self that realizes, imagines, looks down upon the self lying there—the self that lives and wills and is conceived. This is an image of one realizing his own fate, of conscious life conceiving of its head on the pillow as one of the men who by living is dying:

> Yet life itself, the fulfillment of desire
> In the grinding ric-rac, staring steadily
>
> At a head upon the pillow in the dark. . . .

The poet of "To an Old Philosopher in Rome" asks Santayana to "speak to your pillow as if it was yourself," and the head that is on the pillow here is also that of one of the men that are falling. "Yellow Afternoon" presents a similar image of the self on its bed in the dark, listening to the continual discourse that is thought, to its self: "A face / With-

---

[4] Trans. Arthur Mitchell (New York, 1944), p. 307.

out eyes or mouth, that looks at one and speaks." This depiction of another self without eyes or mouth resembles Henri Focillon's consideration of his hands in their life of activity, each one like another self: "Eyeless and voiceless faces which nonetheless see and speak."[5]

In the continuing discourse of conscious reflection, one's thoughts, when one attends them, are, in Stevens' characterization, "eyeless and voiceless" selves, projections of one's subjectivity as though another were speaking while one is listening. Such vague unformulated projections of the interior life of thought and of feeling turn outward to become our sense that our surroundings are a composite environment with a latent character, holding such felt and almost personal qualities as hostility, gloom, vitality, aimlessness, warmth, brightness, and endless other anthropomorphic conceptions of encompassing reality. In a number of poems, Stevens expresses a sense of the latent personal characteristics of the scene of life. As he indicates in "The Woman in Sunshine," it is almost as though there were a recognition of a human presence in the human setting:

> It is only that this warmth and movement are like
> The warmth and movement of a woman.

Thus become superimposed upon the phenomenal world various projections of self, personifications that embody ancient emotional attitudes and experiences. These are the archetypes that summarize human feelings in the shapes of the hero, the child, the father, the mother, the maiden. In myth and art these imagined ancient projections of the common interior life of man look at us in accordance with our desire and speak with our latent feeling.

Holding rich connotations from the long inheritance of human emotions that engendered them, such incipient

[5] Henri Focillon, "In Praise of Hands," trans. S. L. Faison, *The Life of Forms in Art* (New York, 1948), p. 65.

mythic figures seem perfectly at home in the symbolic action
of the poetry of Stevens. The most significant for him, at
least the one that recurs most often, is the symbolic woman,[6]
abstracted by the poet from the ground of humanity's common discovery of her as reality or earth, the mother or beautiful maiden, and made manifest in myth and art. As expressed in "Yellow Afternoon," she is both inner reality and
outer reality, the field of consciousness that in Stevens'
brilliant pun is also the field or earth that is both his body
and his world:

> Everything comes to him
> From the middle of his field. The odor
> Of earth penetrates more deeply than any word.
> There he touches his being. There as he is
> He is. The thought that he had found all this
> Among men, in a woman—she caught his breath. . . .

A useful version of the nature of the image of woman and
one that gives support to Stevens' vision of the archetype is
that of the anima of Jung:

> The projection-making factor is the anima, or rather the
> unconscious as represented by the anima. Whenever she
> appears, in dreams, visions, and fantasies, she takes on personi-
> fied form, thus demonstrating that the factor she embodies
> possesses all the outstanding characteristics of a feminine
> being. She is not an invention of the conscious mind, but a
> spontaneous production of the unconscious. . . .[7]

[6] See Michel Benamou, "Beyond Emerald or Amethyst—Wallace Stevens
and the French Tradition," *Dartmouth College Library Bulletin*, IV (Decem-
ber, 1961), 60–66. This essay is the first extended discussion of the significance
of Stevens' image. Northrop Frye, "The Realistic Oriole: A Study of Wallace
Stevens," *Wallace Stevens*, ed. Borroff, p. 165, points to the similarity of the
idea of the anima to the image of woman in Stevens.

[7] *Psyche and Symbol*, ed. Violet S. de Laszlo (Garden City, 1958), p. 12.

The relevance of Jung's anima to Stevens' image of the woman is apparent in Section X of "Esthétique du Mal."[8] The poem opens: "He had studied the nostalgias," or, to follow the implications of the first line in the light of the rest of the passage, the poet had thought of the human origins in physical reality and considered man's homesickness, his nostalgia for that reality. The poet in his nostalgia for the real had conceived of reality as woman and found (just as Jung did) one that is both the beloved object of desire and the eternal mother of all. Yet she is touched, as woman always is, by a recessive father image (the animus, Jung names it): "the softest / Woman with a vague mustache"—an image that encompasses more than conventional femininity:

> . . . His anima liked its animal
> And liked it unsubjugated, so that home
> Was a return to birth, a being born
> Again in the savagest severity,
> Desiring fiercely, the child of a mother fierce
> In his body, fiercer in his mind, merciless
> To accomplish the truth in his intelligence.

Anima here means inmost self or spirit,[9] and *animal* refers to the body of man. A return to birth is a return to the origins of the self in reality—a return to one's home in the eternal woman, symbol of that reality. Therefore, the self is born again in its desire for experience and expresses the elemental will of that reality to see itself as it is by means of the intelligence of the individual person. The thought here resembles the notion of Schopenhauer that the world as will or as action

[8] The significance of Jung to the student of Stevens was indicated by Howard Baker in 1935. See his essay in *The Achievement of Wallace Stevens*, ed. Ashley Brown and Robert S. Haller (New York, 1962).

[9] The context here is reinforced by Stevens' definition of the word *anima* in a letter written to Renato Poggioli and quoted in *Mattino Domenicale ed Altre Poesie* (Turin, Italy, 1954), p. 179.

and physical being accomplishes its desire to know itself as
idea by means of the intelligence of each individual knowing
subject. The self is the "child of a mother fierce / In his
body" because it is made of empirical reality and its physical
body is the one part of earth given immediately to its individual mind; in this sense, the symbolic mother keeps her
primal being within the body of every creature, or, to use a
sentence from Schopenhauer as a paraphrase, "She has her
centre in every brute."[10]

Later the poem refers to a projection of the archetype of
woman in myth and legend:

> It is true there were other mothers, singular
> In form, lovers of heaven and earth, she-wolves
> And forest tigresses and women mixed
> With the sea. These were fantastic. . . .

The symbolic woman of this poem has a reference which is
not that of folk or ethnic narrative; her reference is to what
Stevens calls elsewhere the folklore of the senses. In the
more abstract terms of this poem, "she is as she was, reality."
According to the rest of the poem, the world and its necessities, its conditions for existence, are implications of the
word *reality*, and these conditions include the fecundity, the
multiplying possibilities of events, and the grossness of physical life, with eventual suffering and death. Enclosed within
its perimeter of individual experience, the self is impervious
to "impersonal pain," the suffering that is possible for all
creatures but is not yet its own. Knowing the innocence of
the world in the characterization of its symbol, the woman,
the poet does not seek what he calls "the sleek ensolacings"
of a conventional religious justification of death and agony:

> . . . Reality explained.
> It was the last nostalgia: that he

[10] *Will and Idea*, p. 293.

> Should understand. That he might suffer or that
> He might die was the innocence of living, if life
> Itself was innocent. To say that it was
> Disentangled him from sleek ensolacings.

The innocence of the archetypal woman is that of the course of nature that proceeds without any untoward purpose. In its course, when suffering and death occur, they are incidental and spontaneous. Therefore, since the individual person is a part of nature and in its real life is absorbed into the fecundity out of which the variety of natural occurrences arise, that person is sustained against his awareness of the existence of death and suffering for others and their possibilities for himself. The thought here is close to that of Schopenhauer:

> In man, as in the brute which does not think, the certainty that springs from his inmost consciousness that he himself is Nature, the world, predominates as a lasting frame of mind; and on account of this no man is observably disturbed by the thought of certain and never-distant death, but lives as if he would live forever.[11]

The same idea of the innocence of nature is offered by Santayana, who, like Stevens, says that man in his work and his life is the child of the mother within him; for all his activity is a part of the reality of nature, and that reality exists for him only within his experience of it:

> The master of any art sees nature from the inside, and works with her, or she in him. Certainly he does not know *how* he operates, nor, at bottom, *why* he should: but no more does she. His mastery is a part of her innocence.[12]

The innocence that Santayana defines as that which has no consciousness of purpose is the same kind of innocence that

[11] *Ibid.*
[12] *Scepticism*, p. 238.

"The Auroras of Autumn," VIII, declares to be a pure
principle of being—heedless in action, without intent of any
kind, and especially without the set of malice. In the concluding lines the music that symbolizes the will of reality is
the very song of the innocent mother of good and evil things
and of all the pain and joy of being:

> As if the innocent mother sang in the dark
> Of the room and on an accordian, half-heard,
> Created the time and place in which we breathed . . .

The universal mother is sweetened, made beautiful, in
the natural efflorescence of things, and her beneficence is the
spontaneity of weather and season of "In the Carolinas":

> Timeless mother,
> How is it that your aspic nipples
> For once vent honey?

The question here would imply that the earth mother has
another and antipathetic nature. The more poignant, more
searching question, however, is that of the old men of "Ques-
tions Are Remarks," drowsy as they lapse into final sleep,
infantile before the eternal mother: "Mother, my mother,"
they ask, seeking identity in the vacant face of reality, "who
are you?"

The identity of the mother which the poet finds in
"Madame La Fleurie" is the antipathetic one, the archetypal,
devouring earth mother, "a bearded queen, wicked in her
dead light." The feminine mustache, described in "Esthétique du Mal" as a vagueness on "the softest woman that is
reality," is accentuated on the earth mother; thus, there is
also an accentuation of the animus, the male element, latent
and hidden within the woman but now emerging in the
beard of Madame La Fleurie and in the innate "animosity"
of this image (the pun is from Jung[13]).

[13] *Psyche and Symbol*, p. 14. For the ambivalent nature of the anima, see
Jung and Kerényi's *Essays on Mythology*, p. 173.

The symbolic woman of Stevens' poetry may be either mother or beloved. Sometimes she is both, as she is in "Esthétique du Mal," X, but the basic image is the undifferentiated archetype whose abstract generic image is a manifestation of the community of human conception. "When was it that we heard the voice of union?" the poet asks as the archaic form of woman with a cloud on her shoulder rises against the outlines of his landscape. "We resembled one another at the sight," he says in "Things of August," VIII. And "the forgetful color of the autumn day" was filled with the many archetypes, the projected giants of universal human images, each evoking one meaning in many men.

The archetypal woman in one poem of Stevens resembles the anima as defined in the passage of Jung quoted above. As a latent feminine element of the self and a projected image of the unconscious, the anima is the complementary but recessive part of the self that, when harmonized with the male consciousness, provides the integration of self so important for the development of the whole man. An image of sexual union of the male consciousness with the unconscious in the figure of the anima may offer a representation of the integration of self with the consequent wholeness and composure of the mature phase of life.[14] This is apparently the version of archetypal woman in "The Hand as a Being," for it is in the latter part of his life ("the final canticle") that "our man," described as a consciousness or as aware of too many things at once, beholds the anima as a separate being:

[14] That creativity results from the union of male consciousness and the female unconscious is pointed out by Erich Neumann, *The Origins and History of Consciousness*, trans. R. F. C. Hull (New York, 1962), II, 355: "Only by relating to the reality of the soul—the freed captive—can we make the link with the unconscious truly creative, for creativity in all its forms is always the product of a meeting between the masculine world of ego consciousness and the feminine world of the soul."

In the first canto of the final canticle,
Too conscious of too many things at once,
Our man beheld the naked, nameless dame,

Seized her and wondered: why beneath the tree
She held her hand before him in the air,
For him to see, wove round her glittering hair.

In these lines and in the title "The Hand as a Being," there is an echo of a statement of Henri Focillon: "Hands are almost living beings";[15] the glitter of hair wound round the hand symbolizes the attributes of life and being according to a recurring term of Stevens ("a glitter that is a life"). The poem intimates in this way an analogy between the hand and the anima: both are parts of the self and yet both are almost living beings. The hand connotes the creative life of art; the anima, the creative unconscious. Although the poem holds the fascination of allegory and identifications of tree, wind, lake, bird, and garden tend to obtrude themselves, any identification made would lack grounding in the poem. Within its simple action the scene is dominated by the anonymous feminine image projected by the self upon the reality that confuses the male intellect, "too conscious of too many things at once." Her hand held up suggests its function in creative work and thus confers the unity that art gives to the self and to the non-human world as well: "Her hand composed him and composed the tree."

The association of the anima with the unconscious is reflected in Stevens' personification of creative night by the obscure figure of woman. In Stevens' poetry the darkness is a part of the environing creative night out of which reality emerges. The figure of woman embodying the concept of creative night is Nox in "The Candle a Saint," and the same figure, unnamed and unseen, is the voice of the posthumous poem "The Souls of Women at Night":

[15] *Forms in Art,* p. 65.

> Now, being invisible, I walk without mantilla,
> In the much-horned night, as its chief personage.

That her place is not merely in outer night but in the creative unconscious is revealed when she speaks of keeping a rendezvous "in a human midnight." Since what is known in the unconscious is the innate, the *a priori,* she speaks of herself as the one-sensed, with the implication that being one-sensed is a condition, a composite "know," and not just one of the five senses that give messages to the consciousness.

2

Only rarely is Stevens' archetypal woman touched by the literary mythology that he eschews. She is never individualized, is usually naked and nameless, and sometimes appears only in the hint given by the use of a personal pronoun. Her symbolic function is provisional, and if interpretation be pressed, she is best understood as an embodiment of an attitude toward the content of objective experience. The attitude is often that of a longing suddenly realized by a vivid image of woman, as in "Debris of Life and Mind": "There is so little that is close and warm," the poem begins, so little, the poet implies, that is like the natural, the immediate experience of children imbued with spontaneous feeling, "that it is as if we had never been young." Then, using the recurrent notion of wakefulness as the condition of man's consciousness, a condition that tends to separate him from the environing and sleeping unconscious world, the poet exclaims that "we ought not to be awake." It is from this wakefulness, this consciousness that mythologizes the natural world, that the symbolic image of nature is formed:

> . . . It is from this
> That a bright red woman will be rising
> And, standing in violent golds, will brush her hair.

The symbolic woman, the poem continues, has her experience in our experience; for speaking a line of verse, considering its words but "not quite able to sing," feeling the vividness of the day as a meditation—all of these are activities of our consciousness and, therefore, of her consciousness.

The poet confronts his spontaneous feeling for light and air and earth in the image of the unknown beloved, a figure that expresses the longing of the self for the reality of its impressions of the world about it and its desire for the quality of otherness in experience. Stevens calls this desire "love of the real" and embodies the feeling in the image of the anonymous beloved. "We fling ourselves, constantly longing, on this form," the poet says in "An Ordinary Evening in New Haven," VIII, and he describes this desire as though breathing were a discourse with the figure of reality as woman. Breath, in that it is an inhalation of the non-human and the real, is "the origin of a mother tongue / With which to speak to her."

The inamorata or nameless beloved of Stevens' poetry is myth in its incipient form because she is a spontaneous and natural embodiment of feeling and a surrogate for an unknown. The image gives identity to the random events, the disparate objects encountered in a fortuitous existence. When reality is configured by myth, the miscellany of things on every side becomes one world conjoined by a latent centrality of being; its shifting appearances are held together by a figure of reality or nature. The woman as mother or as inamorata reflects this sense of person felt within the reality of the world, derived perhaps from a projection of self but always known to be something apart—intimate but elusive, continually desired and never truly attained. In "Bouquet of Belle Scavoir" the figure sought by intuition is the nameless beloved within the manifold of sensory experience:

> The sky is too blue, the earth too wide.
> The thought of her takes her away.
> The form of her in something else
> Is not enough.

The familiar and beloved scenes of life compose a unity that is felt as an identity but never seen as a person. This sense of oneness in reality is embodied instinctively in the image of the inamorata, a fugitive center within the scattered, random impressions of the world. "The thought of her takes her away"; for when personified, she is only a concept; when sought in perception, she is dispersed into scenery:

> The reflection of her here, and then there,
> Is another shadow, another evasion,
> Another denial. If she is everywhere,
> She is nowhere, to him.

The notion of one world independent of self and permanent beneath change is explained by Santayana as an effect of the unity of experience: "the cohesion in space and the recurrence in time of recognisable groups of sensations."[16] The sense of nature as person thus follows from the sense that the random impressions of life are felt to be impressions of oneness—of one world, one nature. For it is but *one* self that gathers in all these disparate impressions and gives them its unity, and the self sees its oneness reflected in its own idea of the oneness of nature. Since, plainly enough, all man's contact with the reality of the world comes through human experience, then the oneness and identity felt within the medley of impressions of things are permeated with the *human* identity. There is a hint of Kant's transcendental unity of apperception in Stevens' image of the unity and identity of nature, but the hint vanishes into the poetry and

---

[16] *Life of Reason,* p. 63.

leaves no more than the archetypal woman as a myth of "nature unified" (Santayana's term).[17]

Nature unified is, in a sense, nature personified, and nature personified is traditionally woman. Even the physical scenes, the perspectives of earth, its contours and shadowy places, prefigure by metaphor the indefinable desired form, the cherished features: "These lineaments were the earth, / Seen as inamorata, of loving fame." Or as may be inferred from "The Hand as a Being," the felt identity of nature is one's own nature, the self projected and realized in myth or in art. In myth the projection is out of the unconscious emotional life, and in art, as Stevens says in "So-And-So Reclining on Her Couch," "the arrangement contains the desire of / The artist." Turning from symbolic or depicted woman (the anonymous "so and so") to the physical world, from myth and art to matter—to "the unpainted shore" and the world that is "anything but sculpture"—the self, in terms of its animal life as it walks the unpainted shore of earth, accepts and confides in the actual. But woman in art is a conception and enters the physical world as representation only.

Myth depicted in art hovers on the edge of the actual— "between the thing as idea and / The idea as thing." It is both a physical thing, a painting say, and a pure symbol of a reality that is, after all, only an abstraction except in animal activity. Myth and the reality it symbolizes, however dissimilar in form and appearance, nevertheless have their ancient relationship; imagined, there is only the image; experienced, there is only the world. Stevens avoids formulation of the relationship of symbol and thing. This passage of Cassirer follows to give support to the faint inference of the poem:

> Thus the special symbolic forms are not imitations, but *organs* of reality, since it is solely by their agency that any-

[17] *Ibid.*, title of Chap. 5; p. 89.

thing real becomes an object for intellectual apprehension, and as such is made visible to us. The question as to what reality is apart from these forms, and what are its independent attributes, becomes irrelevant here. For the mind, only that can be visible which has some definite form; but every form of existence has its source in some peculiar way of seeing, some intellectual formulation and intuition of meaning.[18]

A symbolic figure in a world of art compared to a world that is "anything but sculpture" is very naturally the archetypal reclining woman, naked and nameless, or, as the title has it, "So-And-So Reclining on Her Couch." Looking at reality through a universal symbol translated into the individual vision of a work of art (in Cassirer's phrase, its "peculiar way of seeing"), the poem describes the visible form and attributes of the inamorata: "completely anonymous," born in conception as though twenty-one, characterized by an innocence which the poet believes to be inherent in the nature of reality, and depicted with "eyes dripping blue, so much to learn." As a symbolic conception or as a work of art, she floats in air on a plane with the eyes—like earth itself, floating within the mind at the level of vision:

> She floats in air at the level of
> The eye, completely anonymous,
> Born, as she was, at twenty-one,
>
> Without lineage or language, only
> The curving of her hip, as motionless gesture,
> Eyes dripping blue, so much to learn.

Then, in accord with the ambiguity of the nature of the image as both art and myth, the poet adds, "She is half who made her." As art she expresses the vision or, as the poem puts it, the desire of the artist.

[18] *Language and Myth*, p. 8.

As the mythic figure of reality, she also is half who made her, for like a work of art, the real world receives half its character from the self that conceives it and knows it only in terms of individual experience. This is the major theme of "Add This to Rhetoric," in which the reclining woman, the ancient image of earth, is given visible form as a figure in a painting. The painting and the natural scenery of the poem are conceived in the same mood, as though posed by the same artist. The point made again is that the real is half its conceiver, that what is seen is an effect of the human sense of the world. "Add This to Rhetoric," the title says, and by *this* Stevens means something very similar to what Whitehead calls "prehension." To signify that perception is never a simple mirror of a supposed objective world and that it is always a human arrangement, and an individual version even of that, Whitehead says, "But sense-perception, as conceived in the isolation of its ideal purity, never enters into human experience. It is always accompanied by so-called 'interpretation.' "[19] If this interpretation, this sense in which the world is taken, is added to the idea of rhetoric, then one can consider the flow of experience itself as another and nonverbal flow of meaning. As Stevens himself observes in "Bouquet of Roses in Sunlight," a poem that also adds the context of individual experience to rhetoric,

> It is like a flow of meanings with no speech
> And of as many meanings as of men.

The human sense of the world, therefore, permeates things with human feeling and projects the human condition upon everything that enters experience. In "Add This to Rhetoric" there is also the implication that men think and feel according to conventions of thinking and feeling. Thus, there is a

[19] "Prehension" is the individual feeling of a particular experience, an essential factor in interpreting and shaping continuing experience. See *Adventures of Ideas* (New York, 1955), p. 218.

touch of the histrionic in the human set, and the scene of life is characterized by the dramatics of animal existence. Within experience, therefore, the world becomes arranged, and the arrangement is made according to the worn, conventional feelings and prehensive attitudes of the human self. "Like the artist, the mind works upon nature," Focillon says.[20] Because of one's accustomed presumptions of how the world is to be taken, it is posed as though an arrangement of an artist, and the arrangement is an effect of one's individual and human sense of things:

> The sense creates the pose.
> In this it moves and speaks.

When to this innate arrangement of experience is added the enhancements of the arts of man—"the poses of speech, of paint / Of music"—the inamorata is portrayed as in a painting, reclining in a spent conventional pose under the moon, which symbolizes the human imagination:

> Her body lies
> Worn out, her arm falls down,
> Her fingers touch the ground.

Reflecting in symbolic terms the theme of the poem, the amorphous moon that shows its light above the reclining woman is described as a vagueness, "a brush of white," to indicate the shapelessness and obscurity of mind (except when assuming an observed or desired form):

> Above her to the left,
> A brush of white, the obscure,
> The moon without a shape,
> A fringed eye in a crypt.

The eye in a crypt, to which the moon is compared, is also the interior *I* buried in the vault of the body. It is Stevens' recurrent pun, and he apparently sees the identification of *I*

[20] *Forms in Art*, p. 44.

and *eye* as only a natural identification of ego with vision, as did Whitehead, who, thinking of vision in its larger sense and reflecting on the pun as implied by Hume's idea of identity, found it "the ultimate truth of animal perception."[21] Schopenhauer, too, points to the essence of the pun when he calls the ego "the pure subject of knowing, the eternal eye of the world."[22]

The *I* that is identified with its vision of reality and that projects the inamorata as an expression of the essence of its desires for that vision finds in this image the ease and security that are associated with the idea of permanence; for the image of woman is figurative being, and her constant identity is representative of the enduring presence of reality, the continual "now" of existence. When the image of eternal youth is presented in conjunction with the flux, the serenity of the inamorata becomes symbolic of the world that always is, that grants only the changes of appearance, like those of the seasons, to the forces of change. In the earliest appearance of the inamorata in *The Collected Poems,* she is already the naked, nameless personification of earth traversing the flux. Nature unified has the appearance of a season of the year, and although early in the year she embodies vernal meagerness (as in the title "The Paltry Nude Starts on a Spring Voyage"), in due time and at a later day, she is the goldener nude of summer. The poem differentiates her from the archaic image of Venus (for instance Botticelli's) in that she begins the spring voyage not on a shell but on "the first found weed," the very beginning of the season.

Stevens' last version of the nameless reclining woman, "sleek in a natural nakedness," is that of "The Hermitage at the Centre." The arrangement of the poem illustrates its title and its meaning, for it is a kind of verbal fugue. The

---

[21] *Process and Reality* (New York, 1960), p. 180.
[22] *Will and Idea,* p. 294.

first voice, made of a sequence of the first lines of each
stanza, stands in front of the second voice (the remaining two
lines of each stanza read consecutively). The first voice
describes the flux as a vast turbulence of wind composed of a
succession of gusts, with the end of one the beginning of
another:

> And the wind sways like a great thing tottering—
>
> . . . .
>
> Which suddenly is all dissolved and gone.

The second voice reveals the inamorata, the serene and
constant identity of the world, hidden as in a hermitage beyond the tumult of the flux. Reclining on the grass in the
tranquillity that represents the yearning of the self for a
permanence of being like that of the enduring essence of
reality, she regards the creatures of the world (ducks in
Stevens are paradigms of life), children of earth lucent with
the light of consciousness. She listens to the intelligibility
of immediate experience, the substitute that the natural world
offers to the unreality of thought. The "unintelligible
thought" that is like the twittering of birds has the same kind
of unintelligibility that Santayana ascribes to human reason:
"unintelligible dialectically, although full of a pleasant
alacrity and confidence, like the chirping of birds."[23] The
bell-like tones of birds are pure sound and an inherent part
of physical reality. In the eternal presence of nature, all of
the sounds of earth are natural sounds; thought is no more
than another twittering, and pure song has more wit, is more
intelligible because more eloquent, various, voluble:

> How soft the grass on which the desired
> Reclines in the temperature of heaven—
>
> . . . .

[23] *Scepticism*, p. 283.

Sleek in a natural nakedness,
She attends the tintinnabula—

.   .   .   .

Of birds called up by more than the sun,
Birds of more wit, that substitute—

.   .   .   .

Their intelligible twittering
For unintelligible thought.

.   .   .   .

And one last look at the ducks is a look
At lucent children round her in a ring.

This poem within a poem, formed of the second and third
lines of each stanza, expresses a basic concept of Stevens'
naturalism (later presented in the image of the rock): the
idea of a permanence of reality in the midst of change. To
illustrate this idea, the poem presents the mythic vision of
nature: naked and innocent, reclining in a calm among her
creatures.

IV

The River
That Flows Nowhere

*In the first place there is posited for us a
general fact: namely, something is going
on; there is an occurrence for definition.*[1]
Whitehead

1

"An Ordinary Evening in New Haven" ends with a phrase
that expresses Stevens' sense of the flux of things: "A force
that traverses a shade" affirms the domination of time and
process over a world continually passing away. Stevens'
poetry is permeated by the idea of time, and a great deal of
the poetry can be known only in terms of his concept of
process and the relevance of many of his images to this concept. There is also needed a recognition of those images of
an illusory sense of security in personal identity and of a
seeming permanence of self which Stevens sets amid his
versions of "all things are flowing."

In the scene of one of his last poems, "A Quiet Normal
Life," while seated in the chair of his enduring selfhood and

[1] *The Concept of Nature* (Ann Arbor, 1957), p. 49.

thinking his most tranquil thoughts, he is aware of a sense of passage and mortality, and he realizes that his chair is in a place too frail to support his desire for permanence. This place, "so shadowed over and naught," is the world of process and time. Again in "Human Arrangement" Stevens represents in the figure of his chair such enduring form and identity as are his in such a world. And to give a sense of the incongruity of the human arrangements made by man standing in the midst of the non-human flux of time, Stevens imagines his chair standing in a sky of evening rain. In the monotony of rain and its continual sound he evokes an intuition of the universal flux, pouring within and from without and never changing in its iteration of change. The evening rain that is one continual pouring of time but that begins and ends in each instant is the encompassing condition of the accustomed security of one mind. In accordance with Stevens' usual conception of man, the chair is without support or origin, "forced up from nothing," forced into being; and the nature of the self (the chair) is without any basis, a creation of the human will and imagination. Here, as in several of the poems, he sits amid the enforcements of existence.

Part of the nature of the self is the instant of time that is its present moment of consciousness. This moment, this now-given instead of all other moments—is familiar and appropriate to the self. His "ease of mind," he calls it in "Prologues to What Is Possible," and here he represents the duration of that moment of which he is aware and in which he is living as a boat that holds him in his time voyage. A similar image is used by William James in the *Psychology* to define our awareness of the present as an interval of time. James describes this sense of the present as a time duration in which we ride through time in a forward direction as in a boat. "The unit of composition of our perception of time

is a *duration,* with a bow and a stern, as it were."[2] In Stevens'
poem the man standing alone in his boat rides in that which
is his ease of mind, the present of which he himself is a part:

> So that he that stood up in the boat leaning and
> looking before him
> Did not pass like someone voyaging out of and
> beyond the familiar.

These images of the chair and the boat are static images of
the self and emphasize its continuing identity in the midst
of time and change.

Continuing identity, however, does not preclude the fact
that the individual changes, and Stevens also conceives of the
self as a center of change and animation, sometimes in terms
of the idea of the inner flow of experience, at other times of
an interior person or creature, or again with no more than a
suggestion of the secret activity of life "in the central of our
being." Stevens uses *humming* to suggest that animation is
a continuous inner commotion and implies by this image
that he shares Bergson's idea of the flux as the coursing of
the interior life, of "duration," as Bergson terms the interior
flux of experience. Bergson speaks of the activity of life
within as "the uninterrupted humming of life's depths" and
adds, "that is where real duration is."[3] Stevens' version of
this description of the flux of life within is "the form on the
pillow humming while one sleeps," picturing himself stilled
in sleep but full of the stir of animation. Santayana expresses

[2] New York, 1950, I, 609.

Another image of the voyager traversing time and borne in the boat that
is his empirical moment is the well-known passage of Schopenhauer: "Just as
a sailor sits in a boat trusting to his frail barque in a stormy sea, unbounded
in every direction, rising and falling with the howling mountainous waves;
so in the midst of a world of sorrows the individual man sits quietly, supported by and trusting to the *principium individuationis,* or the way in
which the individual knows things as phenomena." *Will and Idea,* p. 363.

[3] *The Creative Mind,* trans. Maybelle L. Andison (New York, 1946),
pp. 149–50.

a similar idea with the same image, "the very hum of change within him."[4]

The coursing of the interior life and the constant pouring of the universal flux are one. This interior current is his life stream, his own flow of experience, but it is destroying him. Like wind blowing in an empty place, the passage of life is an intersection of time and place, the present time (wind) in abstract (or empty) place:

> . . . The wind blew in the empty place.
> The winter wind blew in an empty place—
> There was that difference between the and an,
> The difference between himself and no man,
> No man that heard a wind in an empty place.

The necessities of being—the intersections of place and time that make existence possible and the continual mutations of the flux—exist whether a man is there to attend them or not, and this is the difference the poem indicates as the "difference between the and an." But one is there—one's existence is part of that necessity, of that blank will behind all fact that is the nature of the inhuman arrangement amidst which man must sit in his chair. This necessity is the element of fate among the contingencies of Stevens' world.

One of the elements of fate is the limitation of the human mechanism, like its delayed reaction in the lag between event and consciousness of event. In "A Collect of Philosophy" Stevens observes that "we never see the world except the moment after. Thus we are constantly observing the past."[5] Considering the continual flow of process, that flow more rapid than thought, Stevens' man with the blue guitar sees the basis of conception vanishing before the concept can form and wonders if experience is only a relic of something already past:

---

[4] *Scepticism*, p. 35.
[5] *OP*, p. 190.

> . . . Am I a man that is dead

> At a table on which the food is cold?
> Is my thought a memory, not alive?

It is because of incessant passage in the present moment
that the world is seen only the moment after, and this light-
ning passage occurs within the life of experience in such a
way that whatever is entering that life is simultaneously de-
parting. Stevens expresses his realization that we gain and
lose the good of this world at the instant of our experience of
it in the celebrated lines from "Le Monocle de Mon Oncle":

> The honey of heaven may or may not come,
> But that of earth both comes and goes at once.

The poetry alternates between a consideration of the coming and of the going. The going is evidence of the continuous
close of life and relates this instant of consciousness to that
final instant. Thus, the poet finds an implication of his own
mortality in the constant going of all elements in present
experience. In "Waving Adieu, Adieu, Adieu" he observes
that even the simple activity of living—merely standing still
or sleeping without movement—is a fateful act, an act of
bidding farewell, at least in Stevens' world, where each
moment is final. All the time all men are falling, he maintains in another poem, "The Men That are Falling," in
which he pictures one man lying down in his catastrophic
room, falling even while he falls asleep (the pun, although
never used in the poem, is doubtless the source of his profound metaphor). Falling, dissolving, ruined, defeated in
each instant, the world is a "relic of farewells."

Yet, from moment to moment, the world endures. Each
one in an enduring world remains himself. Stevens' sense of
time is that of a continuing on, a sense of the last moment
projected into the succeeding one. From the vantage of his
endurance as himself, of his continuing identity, Stevens

engages in the discoveries of the emerging moment. He is aware of each instant's staleness and freshness, of the old remaining while the new is preparing its novelty. The process is depicted as seasonal change in "Owl's Clover":

> . . . It is only enough
> To live incessantly in change. See how
> On a day still full of summer, when the leaves
> Appear to sleep within a sleeping air,
> They suddenly fall and the leafless sound of the wind
> Is no longer a sound of summer. So great a change
> Is constant. . . .

His much-quoted phrase "the effortless weather turning blue" expresses a sense of smooth imperceptible change, an external and physical evidence of the flux that becomes for the percipient a part of his sense of things and in that way enters his own flowing duration (Bergson's kind of duration). Thus, his very life in experience is a life of change for the self, enduring yet formed anew within him to meet the new world of each moment without. This is the theme of the second part of "Prologues to What Is Possible":

> What self, for example, did he contain that had
>   not yet been loosed,
> Snarling in him for discovery as his attentions spread. . . .

The new world for the self that is both one's old identity and yet somehow a new self is a world transformed by some slight accession, some slight freshness, even if only an access of light and color in changing sky and weather. No matter how slight, how unobserved, one minute shifting of relations, one added light "creates a fresh universe by adding itself." The universe that he imagines as an objective and vast quietude is inherently active with power and potential for all changes. The newness, the freshness of each moment and its fresh universe is what he calls "time's given perfections."

This freshness is the element by which men exist—an element that fulfills the need of each generation and its culture to be actual and as it is. It is the perpetual creativeness of the flux, the creativeness in which we live:

> In the air of newness of that element,
> In the air of freshness, clearness, greenness, blueness,
> That which is always beginning because it is part
> Of that which is always beginning, over and over.

In his fine poem "St. Armorer's Church from the Outside," from which come the lines above, Stevens celebrates his own day as a present moment burgeoning among the ruins of the moment after, "an ember yes among its cindery noes." This eternal freshness of the emerging moment immediately dropping into the past is the yes-no of "The Well Dressed Man with a Beard":

> After the final no there comes a yes
> And on that yes the future world depends.
> No was the night. Yes is this present sun.

The paradox of the meeting of doom and genesis in each moment is one of several related paradoxes Stevens presents of the character of process. The old-new element in each experience is still another version. The increasing age of time weighs upon each day, with today the oldest of all; yet, that day's birth makes it the newest so that "the oldest-newest day is the newest alone." Thus, Stevens defines the present-ness of the flux in paradoxical elements that meet in the living moment—the new and the old, east and west, yes and no, birth and ruin. These contradictions perpetuate earth through their reciprocal relationships.

In Stevens' account the continuance of the world is also based on repetition in which the details vary but the vast pattern is the same. In the first poem of "It Must Change," in "Notes toward a Supreme Fiction," the old seraph is an

imagined observer who knows that the world persists in its
repetitions. He expects the iteration of earth's cycles and the
monotony of processes that begin again and end again. He
observes that the odor of violets, the rising of doves, the
booming of the bees are all recurrences. In that all of this
has been once and will be again, it is something appointed,
something decided by the nature of its past:

> The old seraph, parcel-gilded, among violets
> Inhaled the appointed odor, while the doves
> Rose up like phantoms from chronologies.

He sees a succession of innumerable selves springing up out
of history, single beings coming and passing—all the endless
passage of life he sees, has seen, and would see again. "The
bees came booming as if they had never gone" is an assurance
of the stability of patterns of process in the face of the flux.

With this recurrence in process, identity can be sustained.
One could not know oneself from moment to moment if
there were no persistent elements in one's world, if it did
not always seem the same place. In Stevens' sense of the flux,
there is a mingling of repetition and alteration. Out of the
alteration comes the eternal novelty of experience, and out
of the repetitions of one's world, the continuance of one's
identity.

Stevens discerns another paradox in the flux in that it is a
progress that never advances. Although there is one direction
to the uninterrupted flow of time, each moment and each
life are a beginning all over again. In Stevens' sense of it,
the course of time is not that of a development. Continuance
is the pattern recurring, the standard repertoire. One of the
epigrams of "Like Decorations in a Nigger Cemetery" indicates a concept of the continuance of time as recurrence
rather than development:

> Always the standard repertoire in line
> And that would be perfection, if each began
> Not by beginning but at the last man's end.

Progression without development, the new-old, the yes-no, the permanence that exists in change, the experience that comes and goes at once—these paradoxes are the central elements in the poet's concept of process. It is plain from this that Stevens is concerned with empirical time. His own experience of the flux is often given as an open perspective on all movement and change, as in "Repetitions of a Young Captain," in which he expresses a deep sense of universal action and power. That there is continual activity everywhere, that everything is changing, that the very nature of experience is transition, succession, flux—here is the evidence of the reality of things, and here is the strength that upholds existence itself. The assurance of the reality of time given in the epigraph by Whitehead serves simply and admirably for Stevens' position: "something is going on; there is an occurrence for definition."

Stevens' sense that something is going on is for him an intuition of the actual, of some strength exterior to mind and language. "There it is," he asserts of this action and strength, discerning, beyond the simple turning of the calendar of earth, a force-impelling process:

> And beyond the days, beyond the slow-foot litters
> Of the nights, the actual, universal strength,
> Without a word of rhetoric—there it is.

The universal action is creator and destroyer of all that exists. The world of the present is like a theater, with continually changing scenery and constant movement and replacement of actors. The action is both inanimate and animate, a turmoil of mind and machine-like repetition. Change is determined by necessity rather than option, with the will of things and of men in constant effect and counter-effect. He himself is one of millions of instances of cosmic action. In "Repetitions of a Young Captain" he offers as his assertion his poem, his "memorandum verbal" of the giant total of all universal action and strength that are continually constructing all existing scenes and things:

>   . . . the enormous harnesses
> And writhing wheels of this world's business,
>
> The drivers in the wind-blows cracking whips,
> The pulling into the sky and the setting there
> Of the expanses that are mountainous rock and sea. . . .

Changes of scene and person are impelled by a force beyond any description and expressed only with the simple intuition of "there it is." These changes give the world its flow of appearances, its alteration and medley of acts. In "The Auroras of Autumn," VI, the world (like Prospero's) is given the character of a theater and the substance of a cloud:

> It is a theatre floating through the clouds,
> Itself a cloud, although of misted rock
> And mountains running like water, wave on wave,
>
> Through waves of light. . . .

In the course of time, he sees substance like vapour flowing into form and into other form, transformations with no purpose except the purpose of change. "There was a will to change," he says in another place. This is the teleology of the flux.

The theater is filled with forms of life, like birds in flight, grouped, vanishing, clinging like a web.[6] As structure, as

---

[6] The image of the theater recurs several times in the work of Stevens, but the significance of the image modulates from poem to poem. In "Repetitions of a Young Captain" the theater seems to represent a culture or civilization. In "Of Modern Poetry" the theater is the mind. In this poem the older theater with its set scenes and its well-known play is changed to the modern theater of improvisation. The two theaters thus represent the older mind

architecture, its parts are efflorescent yet in ruin, and any
final resolution is suspended by the necessity of change itself:

> The theatre is filled with flying birds,
> Wild wedges, as of a volcano's smoke, palm-eyed
> And vanishing, a web in a corridor
>
> Or massive portico. A capitol,
> It may be, is emerging or has just
> Collapsed. The denouement has to be postponed . . .

The flying birds represent the procession of being, one of
Stevens' many images for the ceaseless activity of life, such
as the repeated movement of waves on a shore, the tumult of
a festival, glistening shapes in a waltz, streams of marching
men. In "Dutch Graves in Bucks County" the mobs of life
are like armies in a turmoil of improvisation, marching without destination, assembling, dispersing. As for battle, it is
not combat that murders; the armies kill themselves in the
ineluctable fate of living:

> Angry men and furious machines
> Swarm from the little blue of the horizon
> To the great blue of the middle height.
> Men scatter throughout clouds.
> The wheels are too large for any noise.
>
> And you, my semblables, in sooty residence
> Tap skeleton drums inaudibly.

---

that conceives of the world as a defined and given external and the modern
mind that has a sense of the imagined world and must continually im-
provise "what will suffice." Samuel Alexander, in *Space, Time and Deity*
(London, 1924), I, 95, also describes the mind as a theater: "In itself the
mind is a theatre of movement or transition, motion without end. Like all
other things it has the glory of going on." Another pertinent image of the
theater of the mind is that of Hume in the famous chapter on personal
identity: "The mind is a kind of theatre, where several perceptions suc-
cessively make their appearance; pass, repass, glide away, and mingle in an
infinite variety of postures and situations." *A Treatise of Human Nature*
(London, 1911), I, 239.

The universal action is too large for any noise, he explains dryly, knowing that the wheels of existence are only a metaphor. The non-life of the dead (the semblables) is set as a foil, an imagined echo, to sharpen the sense of the vanity of the furious and living moment. All this ceaseless activity, this "hullaballoo of health and have," is a constant procession of things and days and men. There are always others, he insists, always "a new glory of new men assembles." And the new marchers are no continuation of the old, for the procession is always a beginning in which the fathers who are going have no identity with the children coming on. The time of the living, the present, is the only time there is, and never is there a duration of progress as in one man's experience, once young, now old:

> There were other soldiers, other people,
> Men came as the sun comes, early children
> And late wanderers creeping under the barb of night,
> Year, year and year, defeated at last and lost
> In an ignorance of sleep with nothing won.
>
> And you, my semblables, know that this time
> Is not an early time that has grown late.

The universal action goes one way from the point of view of individual being. This way is an irretrievable way, the way of the goldener nude of "The Paltry Nude Starts on a Spring Voyage," who even in the intense calm of the present is impelled by passage and proceeds:

> Scullion of fate,
> Across the spick torrent, ceaselessly,
> Upon her irretrievable way.

The way of the flux is an irretrievable way, and time and process go on a course, although without a known direction. When he gives it the image of its oneness, Stevens thinks of this way usually as a river, a flowing present in all places at once and always in motion even though it may seem to stand still in whatever place holds his attention. With all this scrutiny of the idea of the flux, Stevens prefers to express his idea of it in images without mentioning the flux itself. His avoidance of the word so common in philosophic writing is in accordance with his general practice of substituting images for the terms of philosophy. The flux as something named, the flux as an entity, may be a fiction, and instead of naming the flux, he uses a variety of imagery to express his sense that change is taking place, that there is a flowing, a constancy of activity like that of a river.

2

"It must change," he says in the title of a section of "Notes toward a Supreme Fiction." By *it* he means anything and everything and everyone, and by *change* he means the most intimate, most common, most fateful experience of life. *Must* may remind us of Kant's assertion that time is the apodictic mode of appearance, that it is the necessary basis of all experience.[7] For there to be an appearance of anything, as Stevens implies, it must appear in continual modification. He uses this idea in conjunction with feeling and imagery that indicate a philosophic ground rather than a use of the conventional lament for things passing. In fact, the various and particular aspects of the flux that he offers indicate the influence of certain philosophic writers, an influence, however, more literary than philosophic. Bergson's *duree*, the stream of thought of William James, Whitehead's process, Santayana's flux—these were terms familiar in the first third of our century to non-specialists in philosophy and psychology like Wallace Stevens. The basic time image of these men is the

[7] *Critique of Pure Reason,* trans. J. M. D. Meiklejohn (London, 1908), p. 28.

archetypal image of flowing water. This ancient image of time and change has almost lost its metaphoric character and seems now a simple observation of natural fact. In Heraclitus it had been "fresh waters are ever flowing in upon you," and in our age James and Bergson and Santayana use the word *flux* as if it were a literal description rather than a comparison of a concept (time) to a physical fact (the flow of water). Stevens presents the flux in a number of poems by the simple archetypal image of the river. He approaches the image as though perceived by one person or as if in relation to an individual, or as the flux of life, of common experience, or as the cosmic flux of life, matter, all.

The flux of experience for one person is what might be called the psychological flux, for the days and hours of a man's environment create his experience of his life; but it could also be said that the tenor of a man's life, the way his days and hours seem to him, is derived from the nature of his own being. In an early poem of Stevens', "Frogs Eat Butterflies. Snakes Eat Frogs. Hogs Eat Snakes. Men Eat Hogs," a river of swine-like suckling sounds influenced the character of time for a man who lived his life where "the air was heavy with the breath of these swine, / The breath of turgid summer." This was the kind of man "who knew not the quirks of imagery," as the poet put it, indicating thus a poverty of being in that man. And this poverty of being was also a poverty of experience, and the time-stream of his thought (to use a phrase of William James)[8] was also the time-flow of his life:

> That the hours of his indolent, arid days,
> Grotesque with this nosing in banks,
> This somnolence and rattapallax,

[8] *Psychology*, p. 629. James, justifying his term, "the stream of thought," says on p. 239, "A 'river' or 'a stream' are the metaphors by which it is most naturally described. *In talking of it hereafter, let us call it the stream of thought, of consciousness, or of subjective life.*"

> Seemed to suckle themselves on his arid being,
> As the swine-like rivers suckled themselves
> While they went seaward to the sea-mouths.

In this poem time and consciousness are joined in the image of the individual's psychological flux as a river. In one of the "Adagia," Stevens also conceives of the flow of man's total experience, the stream of composite human consciousness: "the stream of consciousness is individual; the stream of life is total."[9] Bergson in *Creative Evolution* keeps referring to the current of life,[10] but James has a phrase in the *Psychology* that is even closer. Thinking of the totality and continuum of all consciousness, he calls it "the river of life."[11]

This image of the flowing continuity of all experience occurs as the river of life in several of Stevens' poems. He associates and contrasts this river with that other fateful river, the Styx. The river of life in one poem, "This Solitude of Cataracts," is a river of time, and the poem begins with an allusion to the river, always mentioned with Heraclitus, that one can never step in twice. In the poem, however, it is the man who, like the river, is never the same, for the poet observes, "He never felt twice the same about the flecked river."[12] The river Swatara in Pennsylvania is a real base to which Stevens attaches his metaphor. The association of Swatara with the word *swarthy* (by its Old English origin or by phonetic linkage) generates a quality of feeling that spreads through the metaphor, reflecting the fateful character of the river of life and time. "Swatara, Swatara," he cries with a quality of voice rarely found in his poetry, and

---

[9] *OP*, p. 157.

[10] P. 31.

[11] P. 233.

[12] Whitehead corrects Heraclitus in *Process and Reality*, p. 43: "The ancient doctrine that 'no one crosses the same river twice' is extended. No thinker thinks twice; and, to put the matter more generally, no subject experiences twice."

his tone indicates that the river, descending from the cap of midnight to the cape in the swarthy sea, is his image of his life stream. He associates the real river with the ancient embodiment of the flux in another of these poems on the flow of existence, "Metaphor as Degeneration," joining the two in the realization that, although Swatara is real, it is also an image and, therefore, a conception, something imagined like the imaginary river of being. How can metaphor be degeneration when the real is imagined and the imagined is real—when his concept is part of him and both are involved in the universal flow of existence?

> . . . The swarthy water
> That flows round the earth and through the skies,
> Twisting among the universal spaces,
>
> Is not Swatara. It is being.
> That is the flock-flecked river, the water,
> The blown sheen—or is it air?
>
> How, then, is metaphor degeneration,
> When Swatara becomes this undulant river
> And the river becomes the landless, waterless ocean?

One of Stevens' last poems, "The River of Rivers in Connecticut,"[13] is an encomium of the river of life. "In that river," he says, indicating his attitude toward living experience, "the mere flowing of the water is a gayety, / Flashing and flashing in the sun." "The river is fateful," he goes on, likening it in this respect to the Styx, but he adds, "there is no ferryman. / He could not bend against its propelling force." Maintaining the reality of his metaphor and holding

[13] The germ of this title can be seen in a stanza of "Outside of Wedlock," from "Five Grotesque Pieces":

> Of our sense that time has been
> Like water running in a gutter
> Through an alley to nowhere,
> Without beginning or the concept of an end.

that his river is an actuality even if invisible, he states, "It is not to be seen beneath the appearances / That tell of it." These appearances are the scenes of his life:

> It is the third commonness with light and air,
> A curriculum, a vigor, a local abstraction . . .
> Call it, once more, a river, an unnamed flowing,
>
> Space-filled, reflecting the seasons, the folk-lore
> Of each of the senses; call it, again and again,
> The river that flows nowhere, like a sea.

The river of time that flows nowhere is also the river that flows through matter and induces physical change. Matter as well as mind is in continual flux, and the flux of substance, the physical flux, is part of Stevens' major theme, "It must change." One basic principle of change in matter is the principle of heat dispersion so familiar to us from the physical sciences as the second law of thermodynamics. Our common experience of this law is of things cooling and of heat flowing down to cold. In *Creative Evolution* Bergson sees this law as a basic part of the flux—that part that is subsidence and decreation of the material world, and he sees all life attached to matter and subject by this attachment to this subsidence—subsidence like the descent of heat to cold. "The vision we have of the material world is that of a weight which falls,"[14] he maintains, and he bases this concept on the image of heat dispersion as a descent or falling down to coldness, a degeneration of matter.

Stevens has written a poem concerned with this principle of the descent of heat to cold and the degeneration of energy and matter, a poem of his middle period called "The Reader." Stevens' reader is one who reads of the degeneration of matter in the book of his experience of change, read-

[14] P. 267.

ing "as if in a book / Of sombre pages." It happens in the
season when the descent of heat to cold is most manifested:

> It was autumn and falling stars
> Covered the shrivelled forms
> Crouched in the moonlight.

The poet listens to the voice of the words of his book, stating
the principle of the second law of thermodynamics in the
language of poetry and with life tied to matter:

> No lamp was burning as I read,
> A voice was mumbling, "Everything
> Falls back to coldness,
>
> Even the musky muscadines,
> The melons, the vermilion pears
> Of the leafless garden."

Bergson observes that the second law of thermodynamics
is physical fact that is pure metaphysics itself.[15] In Stevens
it becomes a direct translation of the physical fact into poetry,
into a book with no writing "except the trace of burning
stars," the diffusion of heat in the cold heavens:

> The sombre pages bore no print
> Except the trace of burning stars
> In the frosty heaven.

The image of the reader with his book of eternal change
brings to mind a similar image and concept in Santayana's
The Realm of Matter, a book deeply concerned with the
flux of substance. Santayana personifies the human mind
and, addressing it as spirit, asserts that this spirit must, by
necessity, attend the flux although it yearns for the eternal.[16]
His point is that the flux results from the flow of substance,

---

[15] *Ibid.,* p. 265.
[16] In *Realms of Being,* p. 268.

the change of the material world, rather than from the flow of consciousness. Here we have an image like that of Stevens' image of the reader with his book of eternal change:

> We may therefore say with more reason that the world imposes movement on a spirit which by its own genius would rather be addressed to the eternal, than say that reality seems successive only to a flighty spirit, turning distractedly the leaves of a book written in eternity. Matter, not spirit, is the seat and principle of the flux.

This is the physical flux or an aspect of it. For Santayana the physical flux is the slow endless change of substance, its continual flowing into form and out and into other form.[17] Stevens senses the flow of substance from one structure of matter to another, from form to form. But it becomes in one poem of his (Poem XI of "The Man with the Blue Guitar") the total cosmic flux that sweeps up fact and matter and mind and life in one continuous seamless flow. Life and substance both change, both are subject to process, and in the vast reaches of time and infinite possibility resolve into each other:

> Slowly the ivy on the stones
> Becomes the stones. Women become
>
> The cities, children become the fields
> And men in waves become the sea.

In this poem, to give a foundation for the flux, Stevens turns to the abstract word *reality,* a term that indicates a sort of base for that which exists or a blank on which time and event come to pass. His familiar image for reality is the rock, implying by this image that reality simply exists, simply is; it is there, it obtrudes, there it is. Time grows on it like a stain, like light growing, like vegetation, moss or ivy per-

[17] *Ibid.,* pp. 210–11.

haps. The poet places this concept of growth metaphorically within the all-encompassing flux and concludes his poem with an image of time as a pregnancy, deep in the dark of its own mystery of process:

> Deeper within the belly's dark
> Of time, time grows upon the rock.

V

You and the Shapes You Take

That any being exists that may be called "I," so that I am not a mere essence, is a thousand times more doubtful, and is often denied by the keenest wits.[1] Santayana

1

In an essay on the relationship of philosophic and poetic ideas, "A Collect of Philosophy," Stevens singled out the idea of the self as one of the themes suitable for the poetry of thought, the kind of poetry to which he aspired. The idea of the self that he recommended to one who might as a poet (a youth, he says) consider such a theme was the conception of the self as the living particular, the pure center to which every other thing was to be related.[2] In such a conception the self dwindles into its essence, that of the single

---

[1] *Scepticism*, p. 290.

[2] *OP*, pp. 187–88. Stevens eschews philosophic poetry whose purpose is to expound philosophy rather than feeling, but he says, "Theoretically, the poetry of thought should be the supreme poetry." The youth is presented as symbolic of the poet in the second essay of *NA*, "The Figure of the Youth as Virile Poet."

point of consciousness with no dimension except its invisible dimension of time.

By reducing this theme to its essential feature, Stevens gained a multiplicity of points of view from which the self may be regarded, with each view capable of conveying the full dramatic import of an existence. In one regard the world depends upon the self in that the self realizes the world as it seems to it, and the appearance of everything comes from that realization. From another view, the self is a temporary item among all the other items vanishing in time, and, as part of a world continually passing away, the destruction of a self does not matter in the vast infinitude of all destruction.[3] One view offers the self suspended in its instant of the present, the eternal moment of light and action, the moment in which all that is actual is manifested; and another view shows the self as a locus of all its occurrences (to use Whitehead's phrase),[4] a point of definition for all the potentialities of its existence. This is the view that shows the self as a sort of receptacle in which everything is becoming what it is while changing to something else. In "Human Arrangement" the self in this aspect is

> The centre of transformations that
> Transform for transformation's self,
>
> In a glitter that is a life, a gold
> That is a being, a will, a fate.

2

For Stevens the self, the single pure center of being, is subject to the one fundamental condition of all existence: its place is always in the flux. "The Place of the Solitaires,"

---

[3] "Description without Place" and "The Course of a Particular" illustrate the two viewpoints.

[4] See *Adventures of Ideas*, pp. 189–90.

he calls it in the title of an early poem. The solitaire or self, whatever its physical location, is everywhere a center in motion in the restless play of iteration and modification in experience and in the ubiquitous wave action of the physical world. The life of motion and its felt presence or noise is presented in an imperative manner, with a "let it be" and a "must be," that suggests the idea of necessity and all the imperatives of existence:

> There must be no cessation
> Of motion, or of the noise of motion,
> The renewal of noise
> And manifold continuation;
>
> And, most, of the motion of thought
> And its restless iteration,
>
> In the place of the solitaires,
> Which is to be a place of perpetual undulation.

The solitaire or single center of being is also a center of knowing. To know is to place the self in a relation of subject to object or to hold the self as pure knowing subject and anything conceived (its world, its body, even the thought of self itself) as not-self. The self as pure knowing subject then becomes a point or center of conception for all its world, as in Poem XIII of "The Man with the Blue Guitar":

> The unspotted imbecile revery,
> The heraldic center of the world

Be content to be sheer subjectivity, the poem suggests, to reconcile the self to its nature; be content to be no more than conceiver of the world. The self as pure knowing subject (a mere abstraction) is only an imbecile reverie because consciousness itself is basically irrational, shaped and turned as it is by the irrational forces of time and chance. Heraldic in that it bears only a representation or idea of reality, the self is the center of a world of blue (an imagined or conceived world). And it is "blue sleek with a hundred chins, / The amorist Adjective aflame." The hundred chins are portraits of the flux of self and an impression of the many selves that a self becomes in the changing tempers of any span of time. The concluding phrase, "the amorist Adjective aflame," expresses the intensity of the pure imagining subject (*blue* is the symbolic adjective that is aflame with pure feeling). "Intensity becomes something incandescent," as the poet remarks in a note on the poem.[5]

Incandescence or radiance of one kind or another suggests to Stevens the intensity of conscious life. "In a glitter that is a life" points out the activity and brightness of changing experience and is the same glitter of the play of consciousness described as tinsel in "Pieces." The random sparkle of tinsel falling illustrates the fortuitous, irrational play of mind, an activity of the self that is part of the total irrational activity of time and change. "There are things in a man besides his reason," the poet says in "Pieces," emphasizing the irrational basis of self—things like the glitter of immediate consciousness or the constant flowing away of experience (the inner flux of self) or similitude of clouds of crystal,[6]—the clouds of

[5] The note is from a letter on the poem written to Renato Poggioli and quoted in *Mattino Domenicale*, p. 178. Santayana in *Scepticism*, p. 35, associates incandescense with subjective intensity. Asserting that the vision of mysticism is no more than an intuition by the mystic of his own inner light, he says:

> The burden and glow of existence which he is conscious of come entirely from himself; his object is eminently empty, impotent, nonexistent; but the heat and labour of his own soul suffuse that emptiness with light. . . .

[6] A similar use of a snow image occurs in Bergson's *Time and Free Will*, trans. F. L. Pogson (New York, 1960), p. 138: "It is the same self which perceives distinct states at first, and which, by afterwards concentrating its attention, will see these states melt into one another like the crystals of a snowflake when touched for sometime with the finger." The clouds of crystal in the third stanza of Stevens' poem are an image utilized by Bergson in a similar vein in *An Introduction to Metaphysics*, trans. T. E. Hulme (London, 1913), p. 9. Bergson represents the self as a center beneath its perceptions, memories, impressions, that are like an upper layer of crystals:

all the discrete elements that make up an impression, the thousand floating particles of unresolved subjectivity, the multiple bits of experience like the snow in an instant's glimpse:

> Snow glistens in its instant in the air,
> Instant of millefiori bluely magnified. . . .

Always the self that is this instant of millefiori is constantly vanishing, constantly blowing away in time, like the abstraction of motion itself or a wind that is always leaving and yet still there. The wind is he himself, vanishing and yet still here; and like wind he is still himself and yet each moment he is another; therefore, the changed self is like an intimate or a relative. Since each instant he is become another, in that sense he is a thousand men or a "milleman" (to use Stevens' term). Losing himself always in the flux, he calls after the self blowing away as he moves about in his life: "Come home, wind, he kept crying and crying."

A passage of Whitehead may illuminate the philosophical implications of Stevens' poignant cry by explaining the nature of an identity that is continually going away and yet still here:

> But our immediate past is constituted by that occasion, or by that group of fused occasions, which enters into experience devoid of any perceptible medium intervening between it and the present immediate fact. Roughly speaking, it is that portion of our past lying between a tenth of a second and half a second ago. It is gone, and yet it is here. It is our indubitable self, the foundation of our present existence.[7]

"There is beneath these sharply cut crystals and this frozen surface, a continuous flux which is not comparable to any flux I have seen." Stevens' image is

> Crystal on crystal until crystal clouds
> Become an over-crystal out of ice,
> Exhaling these creations of itself.

[7] *Adventures of Ideas*, p. 183.

3

This passage from *Adventures of Ideas* continues with an account of the access of new occasions into the self-identity of the immediate past. As a ground for understanding Stevens' anecdotes of the self interpreting immediate experience, Whitehead's account of self-identity modified by new occasions may be useful:

> Yet the present occasion while claiming self-identity, while sharing the very nature of the bygone occasion in all its living activities, nevertheless is engaged in modifying it, in adjusting it to *other* influences, in completing it with *other* values, in deflecting it to *other* purposes. The present moment is constituted by the influx of *the other* into that self-identity which is the continued life of the immediate past within the immediacy of the present.

Whitehead illustrates the continuing identity of the immediate past, which he says is our indubitable self, living on within the immediacy of the present by an example of a man speaking a phrase. Similarly Stevens, in "Phosphor Reading by His Own Light," uses the image of a man reading a page to convey discernment by a self-identity of, in Whitehead's language, "the non-sensuous anticipation of an immediate future."[8] *Phosphor* means lightbearer, and again Stevens indicates the intensity of conscious life by light imagery. Phosphor, who reads the book of unfolding experience, is the self-identity who anticipates the immediate future. The page is dark, but in the radiance engendered by consciousness, occurrences emerge into actuality like words spontaneously realized. Phosphor knows what he can expect, like a reader who comprehends at first sight a new passage and who can anticipate new meaning in terms of the context of his running experience. But as a realist (in the sense of one who looks

[8] *Ibid.*, p. 184.

to specific perceived things and events), he cannot know what specific word, what exact detail, to expect. Thus, he knows and does not know what he expects:

> It is difficult to read. The page is dark.
> Yet he knows what it is that he expects.
>
> The page is blank or a frame without a glass
> Or a glass that is empty when he looks.
>
> The greenness of night lies on the page and goes
> Down deeply in the empty glass . . .
>
> Look, realist, not knowing what you expect.

The self as reader[9] makes sense out of possibility although the page of experience is like an empty glass; and the night, out of which all things come, lies upon the glass, a darkness glowing with the green of fecundity, of potential being. This is a figure descriptive of the interpretation of the immediate. Interpreting the world as it continually does, the conceiving self imposes its own unity, its own identity upon whatever gathers into its attention. This is the aspect of the self that Stevens so often means when he uses his term *imagination,* especially when he opposes this term to "things as they are" or to a reality as it might be apart from any human version of the reality. His best known image of the self holding the world in its individual mould is the man with the blue guitar. Stevens explained his image on the jacket of the book in which these thirty-three poems appeared:

---

[9] See Pack's *Wallace Stevens* for an excellent and somewhat different reading of this poem.

The reader with his book is one of Stevens' recurring images and is closely related to that of the player with his instrument. Reader with book is, of course, a common image, especially favored by philosophic writers who like to illustrate their ideas by metaphor—Schopenhauer, for instance: "Life and dreams are leaves of the same book. The systematic reading of this book is real life, but when the reading hours (that is, the day) are over, we often continue idly to turn over the leaves, and read a page here and there without method or connection: often one we have read before, sometimes one that is new to us." *Will and Idea,* p. 33.

"This group deals with the incessant conjunction between things as they are and things imagined. Although the blue guitar is a symbol of the imagination, it is used most often simply as a reference to the individuality of the poet, meaning by the poet any man of imagination," and we can add, in view of many of these poems, any man with his individual sense of the world.

The self interpreting the world in its individual way is given here as the figure of a man playing his blue instrument, and the specific nature of his experience is the air he plays. "The blue guitar a mould?" he asks. "That shell?" Apperceptive unity is what is meant by the mould, and he is amazed that something as fragile as the individual sense of the world of one self, that hollow shell that is an identity, can impose its form, hold as in a mould whatever rough actuality it receives. Playing its guitar, the self becomes what Whitehead describes as a locus, a special kind of unity within the general unity of the world. This special unity of the guitar of each self is its personal identity which enables all the experience of one self to be recognizable as the experience of that certain one. Whitehead refers to this unity, this mould of identity, as "our consciousness of the self-identity pervading our life-thread of occasions."[10] In "An Ordinary Evening in New Haven," XXV, Stevens uses again his old image of the player with an instrument to represent the idea of self-identity:

> This sat beside his bed, with its guitar,
> To keep him from forgetting, without a word,
> A note or two disclosing who it was.
>
> Nothing about him ever stayed the same,
> Except this hidalgo and his eye and tune,
> The shawl across one shoulder and the hat.

[10] *Adventures of Ideas*, pp. 189–90, for both references to Whitehead.

In this recurrence in the later poetry, the man with his guitar is still there to represent the mould, the apperceptive unity of the self, the element that remains even though that self is constantly changing. Personal identity carries with it a consciousness of individuality that reaches back in memory and yet is present in the actual moment of awareness of one's personal image of self. "Nothing about him ever stayed the same," he says, thinking of the self flowing away in the flux. Nothing remains except the mould of the individual sense of the world. The image one has of self as an identity is an *I* that in that image always seems the same person and seems to look at the world with the same eye in the same individual way. The pun here is Stevens' pun, for, as he says, the eye and tune (as well as the *I*, the player) always remain the same. Therefore, the world, too, holds its identity and always seems the same world for the one individual. Stevens regards this individual view of the world and the identity of the viewer as one and the same, or, to use the phrasing of the poetry, "The blue guitar / And I are one."

Self-identity then is only a personification of a particular, persistent view of things, of the guitar and its tune. By the sound of his own guitar, the total orchestra is known, the accordant sense of the world of all man is known, and there is suddenly (in XII of "The Man with the Blue Guitar") a vision of the multitude of men in their life of movement, a whirling noise all emanating from, conceived by, and reducible to the single life, the single self breathing in the dark:

> I know that timid breathing. Where
> Do I begin and end? And where,
>
> As I strum the thing, do I pick up
> That which momentously declares
>
> Itself not to be I and yet
> Must be. It could be nothing else.

With this affirmation that his own sense of the world, continued from memory into the moment of present realization, is his true being and that his personification of the self (this feeling that the *I* is an inner person) is an image like other images, he accepts a concept of self as nothing more than its own vortex of experience: a recurring idea in the history of thought from Hume to the present, as, for example, in the familiar pages of *The Birth of Tragedy* in which Nietzsche asserts that ". . . we must view ourselves as the truly non-existent, that is to say, as a perpetual unfolding in time, space, and causality—what we label 'empiric reality.' "[11]

4

The idea that the self is an unfolding of empiric reality and that, as a personal identity, one is "truly non-existent" ignores the personal history of the body and its own individual outlook. Stevens, like Santayana, knows that the human body is an animal and remembers that the unfolding of experience is an animal's interior life. At times he regards this interior flow of experience as pure subjectivity—"The heraldic center of the world / Of blue"—but another view sees the self as continuous with its body and engaged in constant animal activity in a physical world. Then the consciousness is animal attention; the emotion, animal passion. This notion of the self is expressed in "A Dish of Peaches in Russia" as "that I, / That animal" whose engagement with experience is a total engagement of a body rooted in the world and for whom even the mere eating of a peach can be an animal ferocity.

"Jouga" is an example of this view that man is an animal and that the world is a purely physical expanse. Here the

[11] Trans. Francis Golfing (New York, 1956), p. 33.

image of the player with an instrument (like that of the man with the blue guitar) is become an image of an animal whose instrument is also animal—the self is become a beast, and the guitar is become a thing of flesh, another beast. The metaphor for the individual experience of the world has turned from the strumming of a guitar to the copulating of these two beasts—the self as beast, and his experience, his guitar, another beast responding—two of a kind, self living in its flesh and knowing the animal experience of self yet "two not quite of a kind." Then, "It is like that here," he says, thinking of the world as a place of purely physical resemblances:

> The physical world is meaningless tonight
> And there is no other. There is Ha-eé-me, who sits
> And plays his guitar. Ha-eé-me is a beast.
>
> Or perhaps his guitar is a beast or perhaps they are
> Two beasts. But of the same kind—two conjugal beasts.
> Ha-eé-me is the male beast . . . an imbecile,
>
> Who knocks out a noise. The guitar is another beast
> Beneath his tip-tap-tap. It is she that responds.
> Two beasts but two of a kind and then not beasts.

By virtue of the individual imagination that is symbolized by the playing of the instrument, they become other than beasts: "two of a kind and then not beasts," for the self is both a beast and not a beast. As a mind, the self with its conception of the world is almost an abstraction and yet always identified with the animal body and the physical world. The idea that the junction of the physical being with its animal sense of things creates something that is not animal, not physical, resembles the theory of the epiphenomenon. As described by William James, mind as epiphenomenon is an accompaniment of the physical reality of bodily functions rather than their active will or cause: "and whatever mind went with it [with physical occurrence] would be there only as an 'epiphenomenon,' an inert spectator, a sort of 'foam, aura, or melody' . . ."[12] The melody, the epiphenomenon, is "the eye" and its "tune" (the *I* and tune) of the hidalgo in "An Ordinary Evening in New Haven," XXV. A slightly different view is that described by Stevens' equation in a letter explaining the relation of animal body and animal soul.[13] "The body has a shape, the soul does not. The soul is the animal of the body," meaning by *animal* its psyche, its life principle.

He translates this idea into the terms of a poem in "Poetry Is a Destructive Force" with the word *poetry* in this title synonymous with feeling. In the opening lines misery is an emotion that cancels everything else in the heart and reduces the self to the changing attributes of its brute life of feeling:

> It is a thing to have,
> A lion, an ox in his breast,
> To feel it breathing there.
>
> Corazon, stout dog,
> Young ox, bow-legged bear,
> He tastes its blood, not spit.

Then, recognizing the human body as truly an animal, he sees the faculty of reason as the man within that body ruled by its brute feeling, the murderous possibilities in the midst of factual daily life; the beast is capable of destroying the rational human temper or man within:

> He is like a man
> In the body of a violent beast.
> Its muscles are his own . . .
>
> The lion sleeps in the sun.
> Its nose is on its paws.
> It can kill a man.

[12] *Psychology*, p. 129.
[13] *Mattino Domenicale*, p. 179.

This image of the sleeping animal that is always a potential other self resembles the animal self that Santayana describes in *Scepticism and Animal Faith*, the self to whom ideas are no more than incidental and fleeting events of its upper consciousness: "but the self slumbers and breathes below, a mysterious natural organism, full of dark yet definite potentialities."[14]

5

Stevens' symbolic and anecdotal representations show that he feels the self to be capable of infinite variations, of division into multiple selves, a chameleon of weather and feeling— one moment bright and single, the next "the evilly compounded, vital I." He seems to regard the interior life as fluid and formless and composing a specific character only out of integrations of animal feeling. These integrations of feeling or specific organized moments of experience are symbolized by the imagery of the body in "The Sail of Ulysses," in which the poet speaks of the self as fluctuating in response to its shifting circumstances; for the self is essentially protean, its old shape vanishing as the new is embodied in momentary attention. "The Sail of Ulysses" compares the self to a sibyl, a personification of man's need to know. Its shape

> Is a blind thing fumbling for its form,
> A form that is lame, a hand, a back,
> A dream too poor, too destitute
> To be remembered, the old shape
> Worn and leaning to nothingness,
> A woman looking down the road,
> A child asleep in its own life.

[14] P. 149.

Stevens conceives of the self as "evasive and metamor-
phorid," a creature of the flux for whom change occurs so
rapidly that the thing it knows is, in the moment of recognition, already something else; or, to use Stevens' phrase, the
self is one "for whom what is was other things." One of his
descriptions of the evanescent self is a renovation of the
Anglo-Saxon form the riddle poem. The self here is the
abstraction of all selves as well as the individual. He gives a
clue to his metaphor and his riddle in the title "Oak Leaves
Are Hands," and there is a connotation of the tree image in
the words *flora* and *florid*; that the self was once one with
earth, that it has its origin in nature, is indicated by "Flora
she was once." The tree, with its roots in time, is twelve-
legged (the twelve months, perhaps) in its ancestral hells—
hell here as an underground place as well as the place of one's
dead or former time—the whole figure representing the self
rooted in its past.[15] The weaving of many arms suggests all of
the activity of the self as a reaching out to reality. "A bachelor
of feen masquerie" ("feen" is a variant of "fen," meaning mud
or dirt) could be paraphrased as a solitaire with mask of dirt
or the self in its earthly body. As in so many of his poems,
the proper names, chosen for phonetic purposes, lighten the
tone:

> In Hydaspia, by Howzen,
> Lived a lady, Lady Lowzen,
> For whom what is was other things.
>
> Flora she was once. She was florid
> A bachelor of feen masquerie,
> Evasive and metamorphorid.

[15] To describe the concept of the material psyche in behaviorist psychology, Santayana has an interesting image for the reader of Stevens'
poem. He describes the material psyche as a kind of bush or tree growing
from a seed, depicted at the same time as an anatomical diagram of the
nervous system. "The soul again becomes a subtler body within the body:
only that instead of a shadow of the whole man, even as in life he stood, it
is a prodigious network of nerves and tissues, growing in each generation out
of a seed . . ." *Scepticism*, p. 219.

> Mac Mort she had been, ago,
> Twelve-legged in her ancestral hells,
> Weaving and weaving many arms.
>
> Even now, the centre of something else,
> Merely by putting hand to brow,
> Brooding on centuries like shells.

The inner self in the rush of time issues from each moment's death; hence, she had been of or from death (Mac Mort) any moment ago. Even now, the poem says, to indicate the swift transitions of thought, the self becomes the center of another world of meditation as though induced by the symbolic gesture of thought.

Among his many variations of meaning for the word *reality* is that of something substantial and actual, that which exists in a physical sense as opposed to an unreality that is only conceived. As the self can know reality of that kind only as an *idea* of that reality, it "skims the real for its unreal." Past and future are both unreal in this sense in that their only present existence is in memory or anticipation; therefore, it is through the agency of the inner self that archaic and future happenings are brought into this present moment, the only moment of light and life and of the glittering change of consciousness:

> As the acorn broods on former oaks
> In memorials of Northern sound,
> Skims the real for its unreal,
>
> So she in Hydaspia created
> Out of the movement of few words,
> Flora Lowzen invigorated
>
> Archaic and future happenings,
> In glittering seven-colored changes,
> By Howzen, the chromatic Lowzen.

The last stanza suggests the character of the inner life of constant change—change that is made up of repetitions imperceptibly turning into something else, as in the change through the color spectrum. The "seven-colored changes" of the chromatic Lady Lowzen can be understood better by comparison with Bergson's similar image in *An Introduction to Metaphysics*. Bergson describes change as the necessary basis of consciousness and offers, as an analogy to the process of change within the self, the figure of a color spectrum through which a current of human feeling flows. "It would be better, then, to use as a comparison the myriad-tinted spectrum with its insensible gradations leading from one shade to another. A current of feeling which passed along the spectrum, assuming in turn the tint of each of its shades, would experience a series of gradual changes, each of which would announce the one to follow and would sum up those which preceded it."[16]

6

The glass man of "Asides on the Oboe" is another characterization of the self, but this time the characterization is that of a universal rather than that of an essence of a self. The poem begins with a reflection on the obsolescence of fictions like that of the personification of the divine river or the idealization of man in the figure of antique gods and heroes. But the fiction of a self that is a human summation still lives in the characterizations of philosophy. The human self or philosophers' man is described as a man of glass, a human globe with the glitter of life of a diamond (as "in a glitter that is a life" or the falling tinsel of "Pieces"), a mirror that speaks, a central man that is a summation or gist of man, and,

[16] P. 11. The chromaticism of Lady Lowzen is anticipated in the description of Crispin's little daughters:

> . . . four accustomed seeds
> Hinting incredible hues, four selfsame lights
> That spread chromatics in hilarious dark.

as a summation, one who has had all of man's time for thought.

> The impossible possible philosophers' man,
> The man who has had the time to think enough,
> The central man, the human globe, responsive
> As a mirror with a voice, the man of glass,
> Who in a million diamonds sums us up.

The human globe has a parallel in an image in *The World as Will and Idea*. The intent of Schopenhauer's passage is to show that the idea of an inner self that is something other than a unity of empiric reality is only a fiction, for when we look within, the inner self vanishes into a mere image of transparency: ". . . for as soon as we turn into ourselves to make the attempt, and seek for once to know ourselves fully by means of introspective reflection, we are lost in a bottomless void; we find ourselves like the hollow glass globe, from out of which a voice speaks whose cause is not to be found in it. . . ."[17]

Stevens' poem uses an image of transparency to convey the sense that the world is seen as though one were looking out through a glass and yet seen as though the observer himself were outside and a part of the scene:

> He is the transparence of the place in which
> He is and in his poems we find peace.

The poems of the glass man are his conceptions of reality,[18] and, when he cries, "Thou art not August unless I make thee

[17] See Schopenhauer's footnote on p. 290.

[18] Because the glass man is the universal human self of philosophy, his poems are the common experiences of mankind. The terms *cold* and *dewey* for the glass man suggest the freshness and newness of oncoming experience. The glass man is numbered because he is an order, a conceived symmetry, an imagined arrangement. The word *jasmine*, with its associations of odor and color and richness, suggests that human experience also has these rich poetic qualities. These qualities disappear before war and death, as in the war years when "the jasmine islands were bloody martyrdoms." Because the poem has been explicated many times, these notes are written only as a supplement to my discussion.

so," he is disclosed as the self in its role of the imagination that creates the human realization of the world. As the glass man is a self of all selves, a kind of summation of man, he is only a hollow abstraction even though men find in him the unity of concept that gives them their human sense of things. The poem sees men in the face of mortality brought together into a deep unity that gives substance to the fiction, and then the diamond globe, the glass man, is found to be truly a common self. Therefore, in time of war, "we found the sum of men. We found, / If we found the central evil, the central good." Or, as he concludes, the glass man in a time of universal tragedy is found not only to be the abstract sum of men but also a true inner self of each man, not only the common realization of humanity by which each self knows its world but also the personal and interior consciousness of that world. The glass man is known, then, "without external reference":

> . . . It was as we came
> To see him, that we were wholly one, as we heard
> Him chanting for those buried in their blood,
> In the jasmine haunted forests, that we knew
> The glass man, without external reference.

The glass man is one of a number of Stevens' figures that embody the idea of the collective self. Still another is the unnamed person in "Chocorua to Its Neighbor," who, on the top of that mountain, stands meditating on the nature of the collective being that he is. As the one mountain tells its neighbor, this collective being is an abstraction existing in all men, a "self of selves,"[19] or "the common self, interior fons." His affinity to the glass man is revealed in the descrip-

---

[19] William James uses the phrase "self of selves" in *Psychology*, p. 301, to describe the notion of ultimate inner subjectivity. It is interesting to remember that James had a summer home on Mt. Chocorua. This fact is no more than a coincidence, however, and has no bearing on the meaning of the poem.

tion of him as "a shell of dark blue glass," blue to indicate that he is purely imagined; but that he lives in the life of each man is indicated by the phrase "the glitter of a being." To think of him, the mountain remarks, is to think of man in terms of pure concept and without the body's specific form.

The collective being realizes that he is only an abstraction or idea of man, and this knowledge leads to a consideration that so many other human characters are no more than ideas or purely imagined personations. Many of these ideas of men are heroic or tragic roles that we conceive as part of the invented or idealized aspect of society. They are images of an imagined specific self, placed in its own special set of circumstances:

> The captain squalid on his pillow, the great
> Cardinal, saying the prayers of earliest day;
> The stone, the categorical effigy;
> And the mother, the music, the name; the scholar,
> Whose green mind bulges with complicated hues. . . .

The captain in his campaign squalor, the great cardinal with his constant devotion, the mother, the scholar, and all the other effigies that men raise in their minds as idealizations of man are more than representations of ideas. They become focal points of traditional feeling. The idea of the hero is another conception that is also a center of communal response. The hero becomes particularized as one man's act or another's person. He is a sort of blank that is filled by one effigy or another, "a man seen / As if the eye was an emotion." The hero as a collective being is the subject of one of the longer sequences of the sonnet-like meditations "Examination of the Hero in a Time of War." With the hero and all the other multitude of "major men," the collective being becomes less of an abstract inner self and turns into a representation of a human ideal of that self or acts as an emblem of some desired human behavior.

7

In his last poems Stevens continues to meditate on the self
of all selves as a unity of human experience and, in "Final
Soliloquy of the Interior Paramour," proposes that this unity
constitutes a central mind. In this poem the world as it
seems to all men is a construct of the human way of seeing
reality, and this same imagined world unites men, brings
them ·together as though into a common dwelling. After
speaking of this centrality of mind as though it were also a
single mind ("How high that highest candle lights the
dark"), Stevens elevates it: "We say God and the imagination
are one." The central mind is manifested within each one
as the flow of conscious experience and of inner discourse on
that experience. It is all the activity of thought and feeling
and inner regard that is the very theater of human consciousness.

Another version of this unity of human conception is the
mighty imagination of "Puella Parvula." Here the flow of
thought within is part of the unity of thought of all men,
part of the cultural heritage that speaks through the consciousness of the individual. This is the inner discourse of
the intelligence that conceives a human version of the eternal
fact of the flux. The collective human imagination relates
and the mortal self listens to the legend of philosophy or
religion or mythology—the meditations of men upon fate
that constitute a continual life in the midst of change. The
poet tells the anxious animal self to attend this great voice
that is like a trumpet triumphing over despair:

> Keep quiet in the heart, O wild bitch. O mind
> Gone wild, be what he tells you to be: *Puella.*
> Write *pax* across the window pane. . . .

Be like the very diminutive of a little girl hanging on the tale
of the dauntless master; be still, the poet says, quieting the

animal heart that struggles against the dissolution of all that seems so solid, the very rock and Gibraltar of reality that it knows is "dissolved like spit in the wind."

In spite of his concept of the mighty human imagination, the poetry of Stevens is intent on "the vital boundary" of self and tells anecdotes of the single consciousness whose imagined world and imagining self share one existence. These two are "the two worlds," as he puts it in "An Old Man Asleep," thinking of the two of them—world and self—as partaking of the life of one being, held in the same state. Here, both are asleep:

> The self and the earth—your thoughts, your feelings,
> Your beliefs and disbeliefs, your whole peculiar plot;
>
> The redness of your reddish chestnut trees,
> The river motion, the drowsy motion of the river R.

The river R or the river are, the flux of existence is the flux of *one* existence. Everything here is gathered together into the solitaire, its world, its flow of existence, its thoughts and feelings, its own human tale (its own "peculiar plot")—all held again in the mould of an individual being and the unity of an identity.

The other view of the self other than that of the self holding the world as a conception is that of self and reality as separate forms of being personified and in converse or correspondence. Two late poems published as a set, "A Letter From" and "A Letter To," illustrate the notion that existence is a kind of intercommunication between self and reality. The first poem expresses a longing for the ease that can be found only in the interior dark that is one's share of the primitive unthinking base of being. In contrast to the darkness within, there is the symbolic light of the imagination, the crescent moon "drenching the evening with crystal's light"; but the poet turns from the light of imaginative vision in the evening of life to the darkness of unreasoning engagement with the experience of the instant.

Whatever it is he seeks within, it is not the self, for the self is forever perishing and ultimately lost. Since this is the very nature of self, he writes for everyone "A Letter From," which is an anecdote of the desire of rational man for the confidence of thoughtless immediate living. He longs for a true interior, a home against this flowing identity of his—home in the spirit of "come home, wind, he said." By simple unreasoning absorption in the moment of present existence—that moment in which all of life is lived—he could find the ease that one finds in converse with family or friends when what little is said or known seems desirable and credible:

> One would have wanted more—more—more—
> Some true interior to which to return,
> A home against one's self, a darkness,
>
> An ease in which to live a moment's life,
> The moment of life's love and fortune,
> Free from everything else, free above all from thought.

The companion poem, "A Letter To," describes the desire of reality to enter into the life of the mind, to be conceived, and to hear the discourse that is thought. Reality, as in so many poems, is personified as woman:

> She wanted a holiday
> With someone to speak her dulcied native tongue. . . .

For the woman, who is personified reality, the "holiday" occurs when that reality is a conception and thus enters the gaiety of conscious life, becomes part of the experience of the living creature, and shares all its inner joy. The "someone to speak her native tongue" is the self, and its discourse with reality is objective experience,

> . . . and the two of them in speech,
>
> In a secrecy of words
> Opened out within a secrecy of place. . . .

What she (nature or reality) truly wants is to enter the unity of the single mind and become its ordered conception. There the disparate unorganized nature of things ends; the circle of the relationship of object to object is closed because it is the circle surrounding that single center, the self. Within the conceiving mind, the woman as reality is enclosed by a land "or something much like a land"; for the body that sustains conception is itself a portion of earth removed into life, and the mind's image of earth, if not a duplication of that place, is still something like it.

VI

This Invented World

*The whole perceptual and sensible world is
the primordial poem of mankind.*[1]

Nietzsche

1

Intent on his personifications, Stevens addresses from time
to time the conceiving self within him as it realizes the world
from moment to moment. "Who, then, beheld the rising of
the clouds . . .?" he asks while considering the transformations
of a "Sea Surface Full of Clouds." His reply personifies his
inner being: *"C'était mon frère du ciel, ma vie, mon or."*

[1] Quoted in H. Vaihinger, *The Philosophy of 'As If,'* trans. C. K. Ogden
(London, 1924), p. 351. "Of Modern Poetry" expresses a notion similar to
that of Nietzsche. "The poem of the act of the mind," the poet says, and
by that phrase he indicates the act of realization. Modern man must create
the modern poetry of his conception of the world. "What will suffice" is the
imagery of experience and the activity of living that is the personal vision
of each man. "The act of the mind" is a phrase that opens and closes the
poem and was apparently taken by Stevens from Samuel Alexander. In "A
Collect of Philosophy" (*OP*, p. 193), Stevens quotes a passage from *Space,
Time and Deity*, p. 13. "The act of the mind" is in the passage quoted or
rather misquoted. Alexander's own words are "the act of mind," not "the
act of the mind." The phrase is a favorite of Alexander; it occurs many
times in *Space, Time and Deity*.

This heavenly brother, the self within him, who composes a certain integration or vision of things, at another moment and with another conception of the world, becomes for him another self and is to him *"mon enfant, mon bijou, mon âme."* This self which he objectifies is capable of an infinite variety of transformations, capable at any moment of becoming a new self apt for a new knowledge of the appearance of things. This is the imagination, the poet within him, the conceiving self within any man. For Stevens, who is always ready for the instant expansions of synecdoche, poetry is the quintessence of all concept, and the poet, therefore, "has had to do with whatever the imagination and the senses have made of the world."[2]

2

To conceive the world, as we do in our precise realizations of it, in our immediate sense of what the world is at that moment, is itself a kind of poetry. In this expanded sense of poetry, the first poem of "Notes toward a Supreme Fiction" can be understood to be an address to a young poet. "Begin, ephebe," the poem opens, and it continues in such a manner that it can be inferred that the poet within him is the audience as well as author of the poem's discourse. The ephebe seems to be a version of the youth in "The Figure of the Youth as Virile Poet," one of two essays that must have shared with the poem the mind of the poet because poem and essay shared a period of composition. The ephebe has the guise of a poet in the fifth poem, where he is put in his traditional pose and setting. In this metaphor of the imaginative self as poet looking from the attic window, the mansard room with

---

[2] *NA*, p. 30. The student of Stevens' poems will find interesting material in Frank Kermode, "'Notes toward a Supreme Fiction': A Commentary," *Annali dell'Istituto Universitario Orientale: Sezione Germanica* (Naples, 1961), pp. 173–201.

its rented piano, or turning on the bed in the pains of composition, the poet represents for anyone the rigors of ade-
quate realization and expression:

> . . . You clutch the corner
> Of the pillow in your hand. You writhe and press
> A bitter utterance from your writhing, dumb,
>
> Yet voluble dumb violence. . . .

This utterance of the ephebe, his "voluble dumb violence,"
is the violence described in "The Noble Rider and the Sound
of Words," the other of the two essays so closely related to
the poem, and it is described there as the inner violence of
the imagination pressing against the violence of reality without: "It is a violence from within that protects us from a
violence without. It is the imagination pressing back against
the pressure of reality."[3] This is "the war between mind and
sky" presented in the epilogue of the poem as the work of
the poet. The youth as virile poet, in the essay by that name,
is identified as a personification of the poetic intelligence.
"It is the spirit out of its own self," the essay says, "not out
of some surrounding myth, delineating with accurate speech
the complications of which it is composed."[4] And just as the
youth of the essay is presented as that part of one that is the
poet within, "the spirit out of its own self," the ephebe of the
poem seems to be also an aspect of the mind, a kind of intelligence within the self, and the one who is addressed (along
with the muse) as both self and fellow in the last lines of the
poem which begins: "Two things of opposite natures" (Poem
IV of the second section):

[3] *NA*, p. 36. For the violence within, see a similar notion in Vaihinger,
p. 98. "The special character of a fiction is not only its arbitrariness but
also its violence. Violence must be done not only to reality but (in real
fictions) also to thought itself. The arbitrary way in which thought
operates corresponds to the violence to which it subjects reality and the
logical Law of Contradiction."

[4] *NA*, p. 53.

Follow after, O my companion, my fellow, my self,
Sister and solace, brother and delight.

Personification (the ephebe as the poetic intelligence, for instance) is the staple rhetorical device of "Notes toward a Supreme Fiction," and in its use Stevens gains for his large abstractions something of the urgency and poignancy belonging to individual lives. Each personification is a kind of man and at the same time a kind of idea. Stevens uses the term "major" man for an idea of man expressed in a personification. Many poems of "Notes toward a Supreme Fiction" are peopled with major men like the one in which man is depicted in his world as the planter "on a blue island in a sky-wide water." Blue symbolizes the imagination, and the poet is indicating here that man's world is an imagined thing. The planter is generic man, but he is also single, individual man and, as such, leaves after death the continual effect of his existence. The sexual basis of human life is indicated by the symbols of a pineapple and a banana tree, and its origin in the womb is indicated by the melon. This is plain allegory brought to intensity by the poet's skill in giving a feeling of a life lived and a sense of the reality of place:

> These were his beaches, his sea-myrtles in
> White sand, his patter of the long sea-slushes.

Man in a general sense (like the planter), man considered as an idea, is one of the important themes of "Notes toward a Supreme Fiction," especially of the first section, "It Must Be Abstract," in which the concluding poem opens: "The major abstraction is the idea of man." Man with his "voluble dumb violence" (as in the fifth poem), resisting the violence of outer fact through his will and the bitter inner violence of the imagination, lives within his own constructions, within the things and ideas his mind has made, like the social order he has created and the constructs of his intellect. In the fourth poem ("The first idea was not our own") man in the abstract is considered as extraneous to the real world in one of the rare passages of direct statement in "Notes toward a Supreme Fiction." Here Stevens indicates that the physical geography that seems to hold us is really a metaphysical geography, a "non-geography" composed of the human elaborations on reality. These elaborations are based on the scene, the place of our lives, but that scene, its weather, the mere air even, is no more than blank matter: "The air is not a mirror but bare board." Several lines later he says:

> Abysmal instruments make sounds like pips
> Of the sweeping meanings that we add to them.

Thus, the reality of this world in which we live is made partly of our concept of it. But its existence as at least "a muddy centre," even before man conceived it—this is one of our certainties.

3

The idea that place is made of an integration of human concept and external reality and that man's familiar scenes are dependent on his imagination is basic to an understanding of the supreme fiction. "Sight / Is a museum of things seen," Stevens remarks in another poem, indicating that the world we see is predetermined for us by the concepts and interpretations we receive from art and memory. Another aspect of this idea appears in the poem beginning: "We reason of these things with later reason." Ostensibly, Stevens presents here an allegory of the marriage of the male and female principle, personified as the great captain and the maiden Bawda, "love's characters come face to face." The heavy tone of the allegory is contradicted by the light touch of its puns, its sexual humor:

Each must the other take not for his high,
His puissant front nor for her subtle sound,
The shoo-shoo-shoo of secret cymbals round.

In this marriage poem as in most allegory, there is an underlying didacticism that gives point to its mere succession of allegorical surrogates. The point made in the marriage poem is an aspect of the major theme of "Notes toward a Supreme Fiction." This theme can be summarized as the mind's share in creating reality.

The point he makes is that there is first the simple act of perception ("what we see clearly"). Then, by conceiving it and imagining it (by reasoning, he says), by abstracting our perceptions, we create place through the idea we form of it. In this way the world becomes a sort of fiction, a mental construction based on perception and elaborated by thought. The point is expressed thus in the opening lines of the marriage poem:

We reason of these things with later reason
And we make of what we see, what we see clearly
And have seen, a place dependent on ourselves.

The first line of this stanza is repeated from the last line of Poem 1 in this section, a poem that assumes that our experience of the world is, in a sense, self-determined. Thus, to know the world in accordance with the accepted understanding of it is to form part of the human chorus, "to feel the heart / That is the common, the bravest fundament," and to experience reality in common with other men. But to see the world in immediate experience without transforming it into conventional human terms is the difficult vision. This direct experience is an approach to what Stevens calls "the first idea,"[5] and it is "irrational" because it is close to the

---

[5] C. S. Peirce's idea of "firstness" as immediate unreflective intuition of reality has been associated with Stevens by Albert William Levi in *Literature, Philosophy, and the Imagination* (Bloomington, Ind., 1962).

non-human external world. It is later and through conception that we abstract experiences, that "we reason about
them" and understand them in reflection:

> But the difficultest rigor is forthwith,
> On the image of what we see, to catch from that
>
> Irrational moment its unreasoning,
> As when the sun comes rising, when the sea
> Clears deeply, when the moon hangs on the wall
>
> Of heaven-haven. These are not things transformed.
> Yet we are shaken by them as if they were.
> We reason about them with a later reason.

This is the mind striving to attain that which is not itself
and, without imposing human modification, the mind wishing the perceived to be no more than what it is in itself. The
blue woman of the next poem is the mind looking out and
wishing to see without the transformations that occur in the
human vision of things, wishing to identify phenomena, to
name

> The corals of the dogwood, cold and clear,
> Cold, coldly delineating, being real,
> Clear and, except for the eye, without intrusion.

Although our immediate experiences unfold within us as
though independent of our will, we consciously conceive
them; we regard them according to our idea of what they are;
"we reason about them with a later reason." Thus, the world
in experience is continually transformed; it is something that
seems to be according to what we consider it is. The character
of experience could either be determined within the self
and be a product of will or the will itself could be a product
of the reality that encloses us, as Stevens indicates in another
marriage poem published the same year as "Notes toward a
Supreme Fiction," "Desire & the Object":

It could be that the sun shines
Because I desire it to shine or else
That I desire it to shine because it shines.

The sun given here as instance of reality is the same sun that symbolizes the world in the first poem of "Notes toward a Supreme Fiction." With this image he presents the supreme fiction of his poem in its opening lines and posits as exordium the idea of the world as both perceived and conceived, as given and invented:

Begin, ephebe, by perceiving the idea
Of this invention, this invented world,
The inconceivable idea of the sun.

Stevens defines "this invented world,"[6] the world of human conception and abstraction, as a supreme fiction in "The Noble Rider and the Sound of Words":

There is, in fact, a world of poetry indistinguishable from the world in which we live, or, I ought to say, no doubt, from the world in which we shall come to live, since what makes the poet the potent figure that he is, or was, or ought to be, is that he creates the world to which we turn incessantly and without knowing it and that he gives to life the supreme fictions without which we are unable to conceive of it.[7]

---

[6] The phrase "invented world" occurs several times in the last chapter of Vaihinger, "Nietzsche's Will to Illusion": "this 'invented' world is a justified and 'indispensable' 'myth' " (p. 342). Other usages occur on pp. 354 and 356. In the same chapter the indispensability of "the supreme illusion" (p. 344) is noted. The chapter describes the world as an invention (p. 353): "and why should the world in which we live not be a fiction?" Vaihinger summarizes Nietzsche's notion that the invented world is a fiction like the fiction of our own stable identity: "The world of Being is an invention— there is only a world of Becoming; and it is because of this invented world of Being that the poet regards himself also as 'being' and contrasts himself with it" (p. 355n). The chapter appears in *The Philosophy of 'As If.'*

[7] *NA*, p. 31. Vaihinger, in another passage that contains "the invented world," indicates Nietzsche's notion that man must conceive of reality by means of his own fictions: "Indeed I am convinced that *the most erroneous*

This is the world that is composed when we reason with a later reason, that world devised by conception, abstracted from immediate perception. From this passage we can understand the nature of the "war between the mind / And sky, between thought and day and night" in the epilogue. It is waged by the poet who resolves the actual into the fictive, who creates the imagined world of our human conceptions. Realizing the nature and existence of that world, now we can understand "how simply the fictive hero becomes the real."

True, in his early "A High-Toned Old Christian Woman," he says, "Poetry is the supreme fiction," but he means that poetry *creates* a supreme fiction. The phrase is used again in a letter to Renato Poggioli in connection with a translation of certain poems into Italian, and its use shows that by the term he means any important human abstraction or conception: "If we are to think of a supreme fiction, instead of creating it, as the Greeks did, for example in the form of a mythology, we might choose to create it in the image of a man: an agreed on superman."[8]

The fictions given by the imagination to life and without which we could not conceive of it are part of man and part of his real existence. "I am myself a part of what is real," the youth as poet says. Therefore, Stevens finds the real to be truly imagined and the imagined to be truly real. Defining the real as the truly imagined, he says in "The Figure of the Youth as Virile Poet":

> It is easy to suppose that few people realize on that occasion, which comes to all of us, when we look at the blue sky for the first time, that is to say: not merely see it, but look at it and experience it and for the first time have a sense

---

assumptions are precisely the most indispensable for us, that without granting the validity of the logical *fiction,* without measuring reality by the invented world of the unconditioned, the self-identical, man could not live ..." (p. 354).

[8] *Mattino Domenicale,* p. 176.

that we live in the center of a physical poetry, a geography that would be intolerable except for the non-geography that exists there—few people realize that they are looking at the world of their own thoughts and the world of their own feelings.[9]

But to conceive of the world that is the not-self as it is and not transform it in our human consciousness would be the impossible first image of reality. To respect its objectivity, the sun must not be named (or humanized) he says, that instant naming it "gold flourisher." It must be realized only as that which exists:

> . . . The sun
> Must bear no name, gold flourisher, but be
> In the difficulty of what it is to be.

The real as it is in its simple existence—this is "the quick," the basis "of this invention, this invented world." Stevens uses the term "the first idea" for such a notion. "The first idea" is related to other concepts of a reality as it might be in its existence apart from a conceiving mind (to the platonic idea or perhaps Kant's thing-in-itself). The idea of something solely in terms of its simple existence and apart from the human conception of it must be an abstraction, a fictive thing, because to assume the existence of reality is a subjective act in itself. This is one of the supreme fictions without which we are unable to conceive of our life, for it is the way we normally think of reality. Stevens says, "The first idea is an imagined thing." He indicates this again in the poem that celebrates the pleasure of intuitive, instinctive living: "It feels good as it is without the giant, / A thinker of the first idea." Here the first idea is something to be known by a fictive and generic creature, a giant, personifying the abstract idea of man.

[9] *NA,* pp. 65–66.

Major man or the idea of man is another of the fictions by which we are able to conceive of life. As stated earlier in discussing Stevens' use of personification, the poem is full of instances of major man. To mention only one or two, in the MacCullough of the eighth poem, "the pensive giant prone in violet space," major man is given form as idealized man. The conclusion of the first section presents major man in the image of the common man with his old coat, his sagging pantaloons, seeking the fugitive items of experience that vanish in the flux, "looking for what was, where it used to be. . . ."

4

The poet of "Notes toward a Supreme Fiction" shares with the youth as virile poet of the essay the hazards that go with philosophical import of one kind or another in poetry. He is pictured in the essay as surrounded by a cloud of those that resemble him, poetic philosophers and philosophical poets, and is warned that his speech and thought must be his and not like theirs:

> In the most propitious climate and in the midst of life's virtues, the simple figure of the youth as virile poet is always surrounded by a cloud of double characters, against whose thought and speech it is imperative that he should remain on constant guard. These are the poetic philosophers and the philosophical poets.[10]

It must be admitted that at times the thought of the poem is like a wisp of this cloud of double characters even though the speech is certainly the poet's own. As is often mentioned, Stevens uses the poetic ideas of philosophers, but almost always he uses the kind that cannot be identified with

[10] *Ibid.*, pp. 54–55.

a particular system of conjecture or belief; in fact, most of these ideas are so slight, so incipient, that some version of them may be found in almost any general philosophic work of the last two centuries.[11] In spite of Stevens' interest in the use of philosophic concepts in poetry, we should remember that the poet in him always subordinates idea to the uses of poetry. *"La vie est plus belle que les idées,"*[12] he says lightly, using French to separate himself in mood from the philosophers who, as he remarks, think of the world as an enormous pastiche.

To see how Stevens turns his ideas to the uses of poetry, we must examine some of the individual poems of "Notes toward a Supreme Fiction." It should be noted that Stevens uses thought to emphasize the drama of individual existence. His ideas express the poet's sense of the eternal tragedy of being, of the bubble of human conception and desire reflecting for its instant the iron world of fact. This sense of the frailty and inadequacy of life in a world that is non-human is the basis of his poetry, for poetry is always a striving to engage that real world that holds us and whose existence is so completely other than ours:

[11] When something specific that might be traced does creep into a poem, usually it is some minor vestige like the lion and his red-colored noise in the fifth poem of "Notes toward a Supreme Fiction" that has a possible source in Viollet-le-Duc, *Discourses on Architecture*, trans. Henry Van Brunt (Boston, 1875). Here, on p. 7, even the lion is red, and on p. 13, the red-colored noise is the blare of a trumpet. Viollet-le-Duc himself enters "Notes toward a Supreme Fiction" in the eighth poem of "It Must Be Abstract":

> Can we compose a castle-fortress-home,
> Even with the help of Viollet-le-Duc . . .

In the second poem of "Notes toward a Supreme Fiction," "the first idea" is described as "the hermit in a poet's metaphors," and Santayana begins the second chapter of *The Life of Reason*: "Consciousness is a born hermit." As for Vaihinger, in addition to the phrases and concepts noted above like "this invented world," there is a passage on p. 77 that defines the idea of the absolute as a fiction to compare with Stevens' "the fiction of an absolute" in the seventh poem of the last section of "Notes toward a Supreme Fiction."

[12] *NA*, p. 56.

> From this the poem springs: that we live in a place
> That is not our own and, much more, not ourselves
> And hard it is in spite of blazoned days.

And yet this place that is not our own becomes what it is only through the human conception of it. Remember that the real world is also "this invented world" and that it is composed in that it is conceived. The world in which we live, then, is an alien world and at the same time has its only known existence in human realization. Here we have the paradox that has given rise to so many of the fictions of philosophy. One of these fictions is the idea of the possible. As possibility, reality would have a sort of existence apart from or anterior to experience, even if it is an existence that is no more than potential. Reality, if it existed in potentiality, would be *something* we find in our experience of it, *something* we come across. The order (or disorder) that we find in the real world, then, would not be a human order, an order imposed by the mind, but would be something we discover.

Poem VII of the third section considers experience to be the discovery of reality. The seasons and their weather in such a conception are something emerging from mere potentiality, something we come upon, a discovery out of nothing:

> . . . To discover an order as of
> A season, to discover summer and know it,
>
> To discover winter and know it well, to find,
> Not to impose, not to have reasoned at all,
> Out of nothing to have come on major weather,
>
> It is possible, possible, possible. . . .

"Out of nothing to have come on major weather"—this is the weather, the mere air, that is our environment and the scene of our lives; and, also, as he says in the essay on the youth as poet, this weather, the blue sky, for instance, is a particular of life as well as a physical geography that out of nothing becomes the world of our own thoughts and our own feelings..[13]

The blue weather, the physical geography emerging out of nothing and becoming real in human experience, the idea of that which is unrealized and enters the life of man through realization, is made by Stevens into one of the most beautiful and subtle poems of "Notes toward a Supreme Fiction," the poem that begins: "Not to be realized." Here his thought closely resembles that of those double characters, the philosophic poets or the poetic philosophers, and yet we can see how he keeps himself apart, making his poem something that is plainly poetry and by no means a philosophic substitute for poetry or a poetic substitute for philosophy. Of those double characters, the poetic philosophers, Bergson is one whose imagery often resembles that of Stevens. Like Stevens, Bergson, in *The Creative Mind*, writes of the possible and the realized, and he uses a metaphor very similar to the basic metaphor of Stevens' poem. Bergson believes that the possible is nothing more than an image of the real displaced in time. It is an afterthought, he says, imposed upon a purely imagined past. For the possible to become the real, he maintains that it would be necessary to imagine it as a sort of semi-reality that becomes real only through the addition of human thought. Thus, he maintains, ". . . the possible would have been there from all time, a phantom awaiting its hour; it would therefore have become reality by the addition of something, by some transfusion of blood or life."[14]

The transfusion by life or blood takes place in Stevens' poem, where our environment, our weather, our mere air becomes what it is in our human realization of it. Therefore, the scene of our lives is "an abstraction blooded as a man by

[13] *Ibid.*, p. 59.
[14] P. 101.

thought." In the living mind of a man, this vast abstraction and collective possibility become what he sees and part of what he is. It composes in our experience of it the items of our consciousness. Unrealized, it can only be characterized by separateness from the warm various human life it enters when part of an experience. The method of the poem is an alternating presentation of such characterization of the un-realized followed each time by a certain experience of an environment—an experience that is something seen.

> Not to be realized because not to
> Be seen, not to be loved nor hated because
> Not to be realized. Weather by Franz Hals,
>
> Brushed up by brushy winds in brushy clouds,
> Wetted by blue, colder for white. Not to
> Be spoken to, without a roof, without
>
> First fruits, without the virginal of birds,
> The dark-blown ceinture loosened, not relinquished.
> Gay is, gay was, the gay forsythia
>
> And yellow, yellow thins the Northern blue.

The "weather by Franz Hals" and the weather of the gay forsythia are realizations of place. The alternating passages "not to be realized" and "not to be spoken to" adumbrate that which is no more than possible of realization.

With another realization of place, the poet turns to his own house among the magnolias; there he observes the creep-ing change of time in the visible. Time, we know, is an inter-position between realization and that which is realized. But not only does realization fail to grasp truly what it realizes because of time and change but also because the image of what is realized is no more than "close to kin" to the actual scene, no more than an idea or "false form" of it.

Knowing that realization is not presence, the poet under-stands that what he is looking at is only an image, the world of his own thought and feeling. Thus:

> My house has changed a little in the sun.
> The fragrance of the magnolias comes close,
> False flick, false form, but falseness close to kin.

The mind's image of the real—"false flick" that it is—just the same is a way of seeing that reality. Therefore, reality is visible. But since the mind can hold nothing but its own image, and, as vision, in that sense, is only the sight of one's own thought, reality is invisible. Invisible or visible, he considers, trying to resolve the paradox: it is there and not here in my consciousness; it is both a seeing and unseeing in the eye. The passage seems heavy in this exposition of its sense, but in the language of the poem, it is light and fleeting, and it accords with the spirit of the paradox:

> It must be visible or invisible,
> Invisible or visible or both:
> A seeing and unseeing in the eye.

Schopenhauer, in the first page of *The World as Will and Idea,* describes the paradox in language and imagery that resemble Stevens' characteristic phrasing. He is speaking of anyone who attains the philosophic view: "It then becomes clear and certain to him that what he knows is not a sun and an earth, but only an eye that sees a sun, a hand that feels an earth; that the world which surrounds him is there only as idea, i.e., only in relation to something else, the consciousness, which is himself." In this view the world is truly "a seeing and unseeing in the eye."

A different view sometimes given in the early poetry is that of the solipsist, the one who says, "what I saw / Or heard or felt came not but from myself." Another image from Stevens' first book, an image of night and of the darkness of inner vision, parallels that of the solipsist:

> The body is no body to be seen
> But is an eye that studies its black lid.

For the solipsist not even the eye sees the sun; there is only the idea of a sun. The closed eye is all mind, and even the objective reality of its own body has vanished and become blind perception that perceives only its own conceivings. The pure solipsist would be one for whom sight is only an unseeing in the eye. But for the Stevens of "Notes toward a Supreme Fiction," the seeing and unseeing converge into a single perception of the world. "It is important," he says in his essay on the youth as poet, "to believe that the visible is the equivalent of the invisible."[15]

Thus, when the poet sits on his bench in the park in the last poem of "It Must Change" and watches the water of the lake, the surface of the water becomes a metaphor for the consciousness. By means of the idea of the two lakes, the real lake and the metaphorical one (the consciousness) super-imposed on it by the poetry, the metaphor expresses the relation of mind and reality and illustrates in this relationship the poet's idea when he speaks of the seeing and unseeing in the eye. The flux, the changes of time and experience, symbolized by the west wind, conjoin the two constituents, mind and world:

> The west wind was the music, the motion, the force
> To which the swans curveted, a will to change,
> A will to make iris frettings on the blank.
>
> There was a will to change, a necessitous
> And present way, a presentation, a kind
> Of volatile world, too constant to be denied,
>
> The eye of a vagabond in metaphor
> That catches our own. . . .

Mind is united to world in the identical transformations of world and mind. The external changes are also the internal ones. The flow of consciousness is our own version of the

[15] *NA*, p. 61.

outer flux of reality. Thus, Stevens says of the transformations of the world and mind:

> . . . The freshness of transformation is
>
> The freshness of a world. It is our own,
> It is ourselves, the freshness of ourselves,
> And that necessity and that presentation
>
> Are rubbings of a glass in which we peer.

When Stevens peers into that glass, he is peering both
within his mind and into the world that holds him.[16] This is
the reason that the transformations of the world are also
transformations within the self. These changes are changes
that affect perception and spread into regions of the mind
that are pure imagination.

[16] For various forms of the image of consciousness as mirror or light, see
Abrams' *The Mirror and the Lamp*. The image of the consciousness as a
flame that recurs throughout the poetry of Stevens is discussed at some
length in the chapter that follows. The consciousness for Stevens is also
a mirror in which the world or reality looks at itself; reality that is the
inamorata sees herself in man's consciousness in the title "A Golden Woman
in a Silver Mirror." On the other hand, the mirror may be the blank face
of external reality that reflects human conception, like the mirror of sky
or air in the fourth poem of "Notes toward a Supreme Fiction" that reflects
back to man his common conception of reality. This is the image that the
children of Eve "see in heaven as in a glass" and an image they see because
in man's beginning "Eve made air the mirror of herself." In the very early
poem "Blanche McCarthy," the world is a mirror in which the self peers
but one that reflects forms and occurrences as created in the mind that is
looking in that glass: thus, reality is the glass that reflects the flux of experience. Stevens also uses the traditional mirror figure in which the consciousness is a glass that reflects a real phenomenal world as it is. In
"Madame La Fleurie" the mind as an earthly thing becomes a mirror of the
earth, and the self that looks in that glass believes that it lives inside the
reality that seems to be reflected there: "He looked in a glass of the earth
and thought he lived in it." Although the mirror and the flame both represent the consciousness for Stevens, it is the image of the flame, with its
implication of intense subjective feeling, that he uses most often. He seems
to share Santayana's opinion on the two images: "Men of intense feeling—
and others will hardly count—are not mirrors but lights." *Character and
Opinion*, p. 21.

5

The eye and ear stand for all perception in the poetry of
Stevens, and he is a poet who believes that perception is the
very material of the mind. Beneath perception (but dependent on it) and beyond the world of fact, the mind holds the
infinite spaces of the purely imagined. He says in the essay
on the youth as poet that "our nature is an illimitable space
through which the intelligence moves without coming to an
end."[17] These are the spaces ascended by Canon Aspirin:

> Beneath, far underneath, the surface of
> His eye and audible in the mountain of
> His ear, the very material of his mind.

In Canon Aspirin's flight Stevens adapts an old cliché (a
flight of imagination) to imagery resembling that of the flight
of Milton's Satan. The Canon meets two kinds of nothingness: the first is the nothingness of sleep, that ultimate barrier
of reality "beyond which fact could not progress as fact" and
where the self lives solely in its own imaginings; the other
nothingness, "the utmost crown of night," is the nothingness
of death, "beyond which thought could not progress as
thought." This is the ultimate barrier of the imagination,
and Canon Aspirin seeks it straightway "with huge pathetic
force," representing in that pathetic flight the human struggle
to transcend one's self and one's mortality by the efforts of
the religious imagination.

The spaces of the mind ascended by Canon Aspirin are the
same vast spaces of the imagination through which the angel
of the next two poems descends. In those spaces the poet can
assume the experience of his imagined angel, forget his image
of reality, the sun, that gold center and golden destiny, as he
calls it. The mind creating its fictions, its divinities, its angels,
becomes the ascending and descending wings it imagines.

[17] *NA*, p. 53.

The imagined experiences of the fictive are part of the real experience of the live creature, the poet. Thus, the poet who imagines them can do all that angels can, can enjoy them: "Like men besides, like men in light secluded, / Enjoying angels."

Here is another instance that the fictive is part of the real, and it is in the creation of the fictive in which the poet engages in his work, a work, as implied in the next to the last poem, that is a pure activity and an expression of simple existence, "a thing final in itself and, therefore, good." Simple existence as a thing final in itself comprises all the vast repetitions of nature, the seasons, the movement of stars, the leaf spinning in the wind. Even the constantly repeated cry of the living creature, "bethou me," the cry of the mind that would transform reality into its own image, is repeated until it is "a single text, granite monotony." Individuality of mind and will is lost in the vast perspective of continual repetition, and the eye that studies its black lid becomes no more than an open eye reflecting the real on the blank surface of the collective mind: "Eye without lid, mind without any dream." The eye that shuts and the mind that dreams refer to the individual mind that perishes, never the collective one that continues in repetition. It is the individual that is the living thing; the generic is only automatic and hugely mechanistic.

Turning again to the next to the last poem, the reader is reassured that the poet finds existence to be "a thing final in itself and, therefore, good . . ." This he asserts in one of the most famous and most plainly didactic passages of "Notes toward a Supreme Fiction," a passage in which the poet finds the occupation of song to be

> A thing final in itself and, therefore, good:
> One of the vast repetitions final in
> Themselves and, therefore, good, the going round

> And round and round, the merely going round,
> Until merely going round is a final good,
> The way wine comes at a table in a wood.
>
> And we enjoy like men, the way a leaf
> Above the table spins its constant spin,
> So that we look at it with pleasure, look
>
> At it spinning its eccentric measure. . . .

If Stevens ever has a moral, it is the one that he indicates here and that he repeats in many versions throughout his productive life in poetry. He emphasizes his moral with his singing hidden rhymes and illustrates it with his symbolic picture of wine coming to men in a wood who enjoy the good that comes to them just as they do the contemplation of the simple activity of that which exists, of the leaf spinning, paradigm of the spinning world. To put his moral in paraphrase: experience is a good in itself.

But "Notes toward a Supreme Fiction" does not end with a moral. In the concluding poem he creates his final personification in the guise of a sort of spouse or muse. The flowing reality that is made into poetry, into "the imagination of life," as he calls it in the essay on the youth as poet—this is his soft-footed phantom, familiar yet an aberration, that he sees as in a moving contour, as in a change not quite completed. Woman is the common image of world or reality in Stevens. "Fat girl," he says, with the lightness and warmth he feels for his conception, "my summer, my night." The world in idea, the invented world, is the fiction that results from feeling and, thus, the irrational distortion. Momentarily in agreement with the academic trust in the rational while returning at twilight from a lecture, he is "pleased that the irrational is rational" (he says ironically) until the flick of feeling, the touch of the irrational, turns the world into the subject of poetry. Then the street is gildered. The world becomes word or, as he says, "I call you by name."

He is expressing in his conclusion, then, the genesis of a poem from the imagination of it pictured in procreant terms ("Fat girl, terrestrial, my summer, my night") through the evasions and transformations of its conception, with the arduous work of composition ("Bent over work, anxious, content, alone"), to the realization of his conception in language (calling it by name), when it is fixed in the crystal of a poem:

> Until flicked by feeling, in a gildered street,
> I call you by name, my green, my fluent mundo.
> You will have stopped revolving except in crystal.

The going round and round of earth in his conception now set in the crystal of a poem, is, like the spinning leaf, a paradigm for the invented world and is another image of what he, speaking of his book of poems, later calls "the planet on the table."

VII

The Amorist
Adjective Aflame

*And what is consciousness, which in the
nineteenth century passed for the only
reality, but an active and burning light?*[1]

Santayana

1

"There is a feeling as definition," Stevens says of the idea
of the hero in "Examination of the Hero in a Time of War."
When this definition by feeling is sustained and multiplied,
the idea gains the verity that emotion confers on all cherished
idealizations. The longed-for idealization is then like something seen rather than imagined: "As if in seeing we saw our
feeling / In the object seen." Stevens considers that through
these exemplary conceptions of the human image, conceptions magnified by feeling and maintained by tradition, man
projects upon the world about him idealized images of himself. The human image is imagined with many gradations of
feeling and idealization. There is first of all "man-man": the
idea of man composed of his basic humanness; then, idealized

---

[1] *Realms of Being*, p. 237.

as a fullness of being, as the man of summer, the hero stands, a concept rising above lesser versions of the idea of man. Finally, above and including the hero is the ultimate idealization: the idea of God as person, an embodiment of majesty. In "Notes toward a Supreme Fiction" the poet says that there are times when man has the need of externalizing a sense of majesty: "a time / In which majesty is a mirror of the self." Erich Neumann remarks that "glorification means deification,"[2] and, to account for the myth that identifies the glorification of man with the objective natural world, he adds, "The hero is the sun or moon, i.e., a divinity." Stevens gives a similar characterization near the end of "Examination of the Hero in a Time of War":

> The highest man with nothing higher
> Than himself, his self, the self that embraces
> The self of the hero, the solar single,
> Man-sun, man-moon, man-earth, man-ocean. . . .

The idea of man, of the hero, of God—all are projections of self and examples of the spontaneous act of personification by which man continually interprets the world. The world must always be conceived by man (by Crispin, Stevens says) in terms of "the unavoidable shadow of himself." As soon as one personification is dispelled as fictive, another rises to take its place, for man, in Stevens' skeptical view, must have something to believe in, and all he really has, in a final sense, is himself. Therefore, there must always be an endless succession of human images, each an expression of the idealization inherent in the act of conception.

Stevens regards the idealization of the self, like that of the hero, as a form of poetry, but for him the supreme poetic concept is the idea of God. Like Santayana he considers religion a form of poetry. Santayana in *Interpretations of*

---

[2] *Origins and History*, I, 149. The book appeared later than the poem. The passage, however, illuminates the poem.

Poetry and Religion says that the imaginative vision of poetry differs from that of religion only in the manner of its application to the practical world of affairs. "Poetry," Santayana says, "is called religion when it intervenes in life, and religion, when it merely supervenes upon life, is seen to be nothing but poetry."[3] Stevens' essay "Two or Three Ideas" describes the creation of the gods at various times and in various places as a poetic act, for just as a poem is written in the poet's individual style, so the distinctive style of an age and a people is expressed in the vision of the gods and of the mythology of that time and that people. People project idealized images of themselves in the persons of their gods, the essay explains, for the fundamental glory of the gods "is the fundamental glory of men and women, who being in need of it create it, elevate it, without too much searching of its identity."[4]

An extension of this opinion sees, in the course of the creation of myth, the image of man imposed upon the natural world. Stevens' vision of it in "Notes toward a Supreme Fiction" is that of a face carved on the rock of reality:

> A lasting visage in a lasting bush,
> A face of stone in an unending red. . . .

The stone face of an unending reality is a depiction of the instinctive anthropomorphism that is man's version of his natural world. Implying that the human face of nature or the human image of deity is a projection of an idealized self, one of the "Adagia" observes that "God is a postulate of the ego."[5] "Less and Less Human, O Savage Spirit" is the title of a poem that asks of any god there might be that it not be human but that it be truly abstract and alien, no more individual than light or color:

[3] New York, 1957, p. v.
[4] *OP*, p. 208.
[5] *Ibid.*, p. 171.

> If there must be a god in the house, let him be one
> That will not hear us when we speak: a coolness,
>
> A vermilioned nothingness, any stick of the mass
> Of which we are too distantly a part.

Stevens is able to entertain the idea of an individualized god on no other terms than those of any other poetic concept. He indicates in "Notes toward a Supreme Fiction" that the idea of the divine man is a personification of the intelligence made of language and the forms of thought ("logos and logic"); MacCullough, "crystal hypothesis," is only "a form to speak the word." Another poem, "In the Element of Antagonisms," presents deity as a sort of greater man riding on his gold horse, "the well-composed in his burnished solitude." The poem surrounds the idea of such a being with a confusion of bird voices:

> Birds twitter pandemoniums around
> The idea of the chevalier of chevaliers. . . .

This image of the pandemonium of countless religious discussions again recalls Santayana's description of human reason as mere animal activity, as "unintelligible dialectically, although full of a pleasant alacrity and confidence, like the chirping of birds."[6] The element of antagonism of the title is change and eternity, and "the chevalier of chevaliers" becomes diminished before the north wind, symbolic of cold and endless time and vaguely personified as a vast unrealized figure of tragedy, with its buskin heard "in an excessive corridor."

2

The "excessive corridor" is the thought of infinity—one of Stevens' many images of a building or a part of a building

[6] *Scepticism*, p. 283.

that represents a construction of thought. The early poem "Architecture" presents an incipient version of this trope in the question: "What manner of building shall we build?" and the answer that we should design "a chastel de chasteté. / De pensée. . . ." The castle-fortress-home of Mac-Cullough and the cathedral in which the man with the blue guitar reads his lean review, in fact most of the architectural details of these poems symbolize intellectual structures. "The Man with the Blue Guitar" speaks of the structure of thought supported by the point of consciousness: "The structure of vaults upon a point of light."[7]

Although "To an Old Philosopher in Rome," with its mention of "the celestial possible" and its "threshold of heaven," might seem to indicate that Stevens is reaching toward some kind of religious belief, these expressions are only metaphorical. In this poem Santayana sinks into the environment of his death; the philosopher rests in the ancient culture of Rome as in a bed: "Its domes are the architecture of your bed." The "celestial possible" and the "threshold of heaven" were part of this environment that Santayana himself cherished even while considering its faith an expression of pure feeling and utterly incredible to him. This exquisite poem finally achieves a synthesis of the imagery of the buildings of Rome and the thought of the philosopher until the imagery of the city as an edifice becomes a metaphor for the philosophic structure of the philosopher—a structure of thought to be left as a building or a city may be left, standing there for other inhabitants:

> . . . He stops upon this threshold,
> As if the design of all his words takes form
> And frame from thinking and is realized.

[7] Santayana describes the Gothic cathedral as suspended on the smallest possible support, on crystal, for the architects "wished to hang the vaults of their churches upon the slenderest possible supports, abolishing and turning into painted crystal all the dead walls of the building." *Life of Reason,* p. 120.

The common structure of human thought is described as a building in "Sketch of the Ultimate Politician." "Building and dream are one," the poet says of the edifice of human knowledge, and he sees it standing in the continual storming of the flux of change:

> There is a building stands in a ruinous storm,
> A dream interrupted out of the past,
> From beside us, from where we have yet to live.

The public or common structures of human thought comprise the architecture of "The Public Square." A building falls slowly as the moonlight (the imagination) moves, swoons as when a janitor (the self, perhaps) carries the lantern of his intelligence about in it. "A slash and the edifice fell," the poem says; "pylon and pier fell down." This destruction of "the fractured edifice" is a figure of speech that Stevens varies in many ways to indicate an effect of a loss of faith or belief in an idea.

If an edifice is an idea or a fictive object of belief, then its destruction is only the change to disbelief. Thus, the destruction of the image of God in Poem XXIV of "An Ordinary Evening in New Haven" represents the disillusionment of religious skepticism:

> . . . It was
> In the genius of summer that they blew up
>
> The statue of Jove among the boomy clouds.

The essay "Two or Three Ideas" employs the same trope: "To see the gods dispelled in mid-air and dissolve like clouds is one of the great human experiences."[8] In the poem, it takes all day to quiet the sky and fill its emptiness with a new beginning ("Incomincia"), a new era of thought and belief. The inference to be made from this poem is that the empti-

[8] *OP*, p. 206.

ness must be filled and the destruction of one belief must be succeeded by the erection of another.

Another variation on this trope of the destruction of belief is that of the death of Satan, who in "Esthétique du Mal" is destroyed by "a capital negation," by a loss of credence in his existence that is as fatal as capital punishment. There is also the death by skepticism of the gods and of Phoebus in the first poem of "Notes toward a Supreme Fiction": "The death of one god is the death of all" and "Phoebus is dead, ephebe." According to this notion, God is a pure concept that dies when faith is gone. The wording and its special meaning were given general currency by Nietzsche's "God is dead." The wording recalls the refrain from Bion's "Lament for Adonis" ("Adonis he is dead"), a refrain adapted from the ritual cry of the worshippers of Adonis. The rites of Adonis included a mourning procession for the slain god. "God's Funeral," by Thomas Hardy, uses both the notion that God dies when faith is gone and the funeral procession of mourners for God, now dead because of their loss of credence. Stevens, too, has written his version of "God's Funeral," and he gave it the title "Cortège for Rosenbloom." Stevens' mock-elegiac tone contrasts strongly with Hardy's rather confused and heavy manner. The poem opens without identification of either the deceased or the mourners, yet with ironic characterizations of both:

> Now, the wry Rosenbloom is dead
> And his finical carriers tread,
> On a hundred legs, the tread
> Of the dead.
> Rosenbloom is dead.

The serio-comic effects hide the true import of "Cortège for Rosenbloom." The poem is clarified when read with Hardy's "God's Funeral" in mind. Then Rosenbloom emerges as the rose in bloom of Christian symbolism and the cortège, like that of Hardy's "slowly-stepping train," is made

up of the faithful who have lost faith, "the infants of mis-
anthropes / And the infants of nothingness," children of
emptiness and atheism and misanthropy. The carriers of
Rosenbloom, his pallbearers, are finical in that they are the
hair-splitters. The characterization of Rosenbloom as wry
and wizened implies a diminished concept of God. The
confused clamor of skeptical disputation accompanies the
steps of the mourners:

> To a jangle of doom
> And a jumble of words
> Of the intense poem
> Of the strictest prose
> Of Rosenbloom.

> And they bury him there,
> Body and soul,
> In a place in the sky.
> The lamentable tread!
> Rosenbloom is dead.

To speak of the "poem" of Rosenbloom echoes Stevens' statement that the idea of God is "the supreme poetic idea." By
contrast, the "prose" of Rosenbloom is the fact of a dead faith
and the fact of a dead Rosenbloom. Since both body and
soul are buried, there can be no resurrection. The "place in
the sky" is the tomb of heaven, as the title and context of
another poem, "Of Heaven Considered as a Tomb," would
suggest. The conclusion is a variation of the antique ritual
lament inherited by the romantic elegy ("Adonais, he is
dead") and handed on by Nietzsche's and Hardy's metaphors.
Adonis is dead, God is dead, Rosenbloom is dead.

Following this skeptical lead, Stevens would naturally bury
any notion of an afterlife with Rosenbloom. When he
does consider heaven, he considers it to be a tomb, as mentioned above. In the formal and poignant poem "Of Heaven
Considered as a Tomb," the stars in movement across the
night sky become metaphorically the ghosts of those with

faith in heaven who seek with lanterns for whatever it is they wish to find, the implication being that they would not be able to know exactly what that could be. Each day the stars vanish as sign of the passage of life into nothingness, and the poet asks if each night foretells

> . . . the one abysmal night,
> When the host shall no more wander, nor the light
> Of the steadfast lanterns creep across the dark?

Dismissing all absolutes as fictive, Stevens' skepticism is compelled to seek finality and yet continually find only symbolic ultimates—final silence, primordial night, the black blank of nothingness. The personal God, eternal personal being—traditional subjects of hope and belief—are sought and disallowed as incredible. Even that most haunting theme of all poetry, the poet's mortality, undergoes the search that his skepticism presses on his least surmise. Looking on the nature of that mortality in "Gallant Château," seeking for death asleep in its eternal bed (thus bringing to mind with dreadful irony the tale of the Sleeping Beauty), he comes upon the symbol of nothingness, the empty bed:

> Is it bad to have come here
> And to have found the bed empty?
>
> One might have found tragic hair,
> Bitter eyes, hands hostile and cold.
>
> There might have been a light on a book
> Lighting a pitiless verse or two.
>
> There might have been the immense solitude
> Of the wind upon the curtains.
>
> Pitiless verse? A few words tuned
> And tuned and tuned and tuned.
>
> It is good. The bed is empty,
> The curtains are stiff and prim and still.

an individual will, for in the imagined ideal or the imagined world of a conception, "the point of vision and desire are the same." Desire, or the imagination or the violence within or the glitter of life or the actual candle are all versions of the individual will, of its subjective, creative energy. This poem maintains that desire set deeply in the nature of the self is unappeasable; for subjectivity is essentially a kind of incompleteness, and whatever it formulates or gains is lost that instant in the flux. Therefore, the life of the self is an incessant effort to assuage its desire or its lack or its need or, to use the word Stevens seems to prefer, its poverty. Desire is constant, and regardless of the apparent fulfillment experience should give, the self lives

> Always in emptiness that would be filled,
> In denial that cannot contain its blood,
> A porcelain, as yet in the bats thereof.

The poem's first illustration of the identity of vision and desire is the conception of the divine hero, "the hero of midnight," archetypal image of the idealized and enduring human self. The continuing conceptual life of the self in the midst of universal night is the heroism at midnight although the image projected by desire is that of divinity to whom we pray on an elevation of thought which we have made out of the stones, the reality perhaps at hand:

> The point of vision and desire are the same.
> It is to the hero of midnight that we pray
> On a hill of stones to make beau mont thereof.[10]

Although the hero of midnight may seem to be a theological figure, a survey of the whole body of Stevens' poetry will

---

[10] Santayana uses an image of a divine symbol on a summit of stones— here the stones of an edifice. In praise of the idea of the existential basis of things of Parmenides, he says: "no one else has been willing to demolish all the scaffolding and all the stones of his edifice, hoping still to retain the sublime symbol which he had planted on the summit." *Life of Reason*, p. 120.

show that, as usual, this is an elliptical reference to the familiar philosophic notion of the generic self. As Stevens says of his substitution of the self for the gods:

> There was always in every man the increasingly human self, which instead of remaining the observer, the non-participant, the delinquent, became constantly more and more all there was or so it seemed; and whether it was so or merely seemed so still left it for him to resolve life and the world in his own terms.[11]

The poem is addressed to the universal and continuing self of man—what he calls elsewhere "the self of selves" and calls here "ancientest saint ablaze with ancientest truth." The saint ablaze recalls the title of an earlier poem, "The Candle a Saint," and also the characterization of the generic self as "the inner saint." Stevens beatifies the self because, as he so often says, the creation of the world in language and conception by the imagination is a creation of reality. The self lives a life of service to the imagination, and ". . . we say God and the imagination are one." The candle ablaze with conscious life is one of Stevens' recurring images of selfhood, for instance, the candle that burned alone in "Valley Candle," "the scholar of one candle" of "The Auroras of Autumn," and the real person with his created, contrived imaginings: "his actual candle blazed with artifice." Man conceived as a candle is part of the common stock of metaphors. Santayana uses the image to illustrate his contention that spirit is mind, no thing in itself but only an activity of conception, "so that (if I may parody Aristotle), if a candle were a living being, wax would be its substance and light its spirit."[12]

The intensity of the imagination is incandescent according to a note by Stevens on the phrase "the amorist Adjective

---

[11] *OP*, p. 207.
[12] *Scepticism*, p. 217.

aflame,"[13] and the blue flame of the imagination is the amorist, the lover. "Notes toward a Supreme Fiction" describes it as "the lover that lies within." The individual imagination is also "the interior paramour," for the consciousness is the ardent lover of reality in Stevens' poetry. The poet speaks of his perception of form and fragrance as "love of the real" and says that green, the color of natural growth, is "the signal / To the lover." In "Esthétique du Mal" the consciousness is personified as "the Spaniard of the rose," who each time he sees the beloved, the real—here the rose is its symbol—rescues it from the unrealized world of things merely possible for experience, rescues it from "nature," so that it may exist in individual experience, in the special vision of the self: "exist in his own especial eye." Again, the pun recurs that equates self with vision. As lover, the consciousness is a male principle; the reality that the consciousness longs for is reality personified as the woman. "The Auroras of Autumn," IV, with a slight modification of these symbolic forms, personifies the human consciousness as the father. The father represents continuing and collective human cognition here:

> . . . The father sits
> In space, wherever he sits, of bleak regard,
>
> As one that is strong in the bushes of his eyes.

The strength of eye is not only that of vision but of subjectivity and individuation according to this recurrent pun. And for the father, who is the ever-present and universal intelligence, the "no" of the flux, its cancellings and negations, are never final. He rejects the "no," the passage of things, and looks to the "yes," to the fresh and oncoming, measuring, as the poem says, "the velocities of change." "He leaps from heaven to heaven," or he sits in almost static con-

[13] *Mattino Domenicale*, pp. 177-78.

templation, "in quiet and green-a-day," or "he assumes the great speeds of space." All of these images indicate the shifting rapidity of the imagination that is arbitrary and independent of the external velocities of time and change. The lowest ear, the physical, hears its own subliminal music of will or feeling. The highest eye, the collective imagination, realizes the forms of vision, the personations, the people emerging out of the evening, or creative dark:

> He assumes the great speeds of space and flutters them
> From cloud to cloudless, cloudless to keen clear
>
> In flights of eye and ear, the highest eye
> And the lowest ear, the deep ear that discerns,
> At evening, things that attend it until it hears
>
> The supernatural preludes of its own,
> At the moment when the angelic eye defines
> Its actors approaching, in company, in their masks.

Stevens seems to have a notion of the self as a focus upon the real and one that formulates reality, brings the light of intelligence to bear until the unformulated becomes "the bright obvious" forms realized in consciousness. For him there is a kind of sanctity and a heroism involved in this art of human imagination. The self of each man is depicted as a candle with his consciousness a blue flame blazing with the artifice of conception. He also sees the mind-world relationship as that of the lover and his beloved and conceives of the intelligence related to the reality of the world in traditional father-mother imagery.

4

Stevens contends that the mind-world relationship is falsely conceived when human will is imagined as capable of dominating the course of nature. The will of man becomes pre-

tentious when he assumes that he can substitute his will for
the universal will and control the creative flux with an image
of himself. This is the fallacy, as Stevens sees it, of institu-
tionalized religion, and he personifies it as an early American
President in "Notes toward a Supreme Fiction." "The
President ordains the bee to be / Immortal," the poem opens,
mixing its irony with an overt pun on bee and individual
being or self. The President has apples or offerings, barefoot
servants or priests, the pomp of blowing flags, and the order
that is no more than neat housekeeping. The curtains sym-
bolizing the cosmic flux are adjusted by the servants to a
metaphysical exactness. What does all this ordaining of individual immortality by the President, the poem asks, have to
do with the endless succession of individual being, the continual beginning over and over in accordance with the nature
of the flux—a beginning, not a return, not a resuming? The
poem points to the contrast with the use of inner rhyme:

> . . . this beginning, not resuming, this
> Booming and booming of the new-come bee.

This perpetual seriality of being is the nature of process.
And within each separate being, within the single consciousness, the world is variously and continually realized by a
concretion of the possibility it holds for individual experience. Even in one of the very early poems, "Blanche Mc-
Carthy," Stevens speaks to the self, to a person, any person,
and says, in effect, look out at the external world and you
look within your own creative dark. Look at the sky that is
only a mirror of your dark inner being and see what is emerging from yourself. The events of nature and life reflected
there, even though self-revealed, are beyond the comprehension of that self, even beyond its expectation:

> Look in the terrible mirror of the sky.
> See how the absent moon waits in a glade

> Of your dark self, and how the wings of stars,
> Upward, from unimagined coverts, fly.

For Stevens the interior dark of self is a subjective nucleus of primordial night: "Night and the imagination being one." Out of this tiny night of creativity emerge all the configurations of events and all the relations of things in consciousness, for the world must be realized to become the concretion that it is in experience. In the early poem "Nomad Exquisite," the physical world is created out of the immense dew, which by association with dawn is symbolic of physical creation. Physical creation is described as analogous to the creation of experience within the self: the profusion of the external world is evinced in the careless profusion of the forms of experience within the self (the "Nomad Exquisite"):

> So, in me, come flinging
> Forms, flames, and the flakes of flames.

Burgeoning within and projected without, the self creates the nature of its occurrences through its individual vision of things. One poem, "The Pure Good of Theory," speaking of ideal man as an instance of all men, says that "his mind made morning / As he slept," for the individual flow of consciousness issues out of the darkness of interior night, out of the unconscious. The content of unfolding experience is an organization by will and by preconcept of what might be in accordance with what apparently has been. In terms of this notion of experience as a concretion, an integration of the possible, the world emerges for the self in its own *sense* of the world, for the subjective will or imagination finds reality formulated in the specific incidents of its own life and in its own vision of things—in *this* world of *this* moment in *this* event. In his dialogue with the woman of "Sunday Morning," the poet asks her "what is divinity" if it cannot be manifested in the real world of immediate sight and feeling. Answering himself, he asserts that the self realizing its particulars of experience manifests the creative force of subjectivity, and this creative act of the imagination within is an act of divinity whose moment of grace is the moment of life and reality for the individual realizing it:

> Divinity must live within herself:
> Passions of rain, or moods in falling snow;
> Grievings in loneliness, or unsubdued
> Elations when the forest blooms; gusty
> Emotions on wet roads on autumn nights;
> All pleasures and all pains, remembering
> The bough of summer and the winter branch.
> These are the measures destined for her soul.

This passage from "Sunday Morning" is germinal, and from it comes the later conception of an experience as a concretion of unorganized and potential reality. The cryptic phrase from "The Man with the Blue Guitar," XIII, "the amorist Adjective aflame," with the initial letter of the word *Adjective* capitalized as though it were the name of a deity, suggests that the ability to conceive is the divinity that must lie within. Stevens himself explains that the "Adjective" is the symbolic color blue and that the whole phrase refers to the intensity of subjectivity.[14] Since it is within the self that divinity must lie, as "Sunday Morning" affirms, then divinity is manifested in the blue flame of individual consciousness ablaze with uprushing experience. The adjective is more than the symbolic color of the inner vision of man, for the function of an adjective is to determine, to make concrete. The adjective effects specification within open possibility. A particular sense of things is a result of modification of the definition of a potential.

"The commodious adjective" of "An Ordinary Evening in New Haven," XIV, holds similar implications. This poem

14 *Ibid.*

establishes an analogy between the need for reality and the need for life by giving the same name to man and tree. In each case the need is indicated as the need for that which supports continuing existence whether the support be water for a tree or realization for a man:

> The dry eucalyptus seeks god in the rainy cloud.
> Professor Eucalyptus of New Haven seeks him
> In New Haven with an eye that does not look
>
> Beyond the object. . . .

Tree and man seek what is the basic need of life: for one, the rain; for the other, the world of objects that is the support of life and its experiences. And it is the definition of that world as a specific occurrence, "the commodious adjective," that is divinity manifested—divinity that creates out of the cloud of possibility the life-sustaining integrations of realization:

> It is a choice of the commodious adjective
> For what he sees, it comes in the end to that:
>
> The description that makes it divinity. . . .

Stevens' apotheosis of the continuing human consciousness receives its most explicit statement in "Final Soliloquy of the Interior Paramour." "The central mind" that the poem acclaims is the totality of immediate human consciousness, which, considered as one inclusive light, composes the moment of existence:

> How high that highest candle lights the dark.
>
> Out of this same light, out of the central mind,
> We make a dwelling in the evening air,
> In which being there together is enough.

The dwelling is a structure of thought, the world imagined and, therefore, the common space of men seeing and knowing the same world. Resting within this dwelling, this room, one can, even if "for small reason" (considering the fugitive moment of life and the fictive nature of thought), believe that "the world imagined is the ultimate good." The imagination, by its formulation of reality out of possibility, creates for each man the existent in thought and feeling, even the place as it is where he finds himself; therefore, the poet observes: "We say God and the imagination are one."

Assuming that they *are* one, "The Auroras of Autumn," VII, depicts an all-embracing imagination, a bodiless mind that creates the world by the conceiving of it:

> Is there an imagination that sits enthroned
> As grim as it is benevolent . . .

The irony with which the poet regards this personification is disclosed in the concluding lines, for the enthroned imagination must continue to imagine, to search, to try out its different persons and worlds, creating and destroying until it too is destroyed—say, by something slight like the sudden skepticism of its creatures: "a flippant communication under the moon."

Beyond and behind the human imagination, Stevens can conjecture no more than the image of a non-human and awesome light before which man holds his little candle and its tiny flame of consciousness—the "arctic effulgence" of "The Auroras of Autumn."[15] In a different mood, "Contrary Thesis (II)" gives an account of the experience of a man walking in the autumn park and suddenly having a sense of a world-ground, an abstraction that is

> The premiss from which all things were conclusions,
> The noble, Alexandrine verve. . . .

It was there—"an abstract, of which the sun, the dog, the boy / Were contours"—and it was suddenly gone again, leav-

[15] The word recalls the image of Jacob Boehme in the title of his book *Aurora*.

ing only an immediate perception of the simple scene: the park with the Negroes playing football.

The aurora and the abstract in these two poems are an intuition of the noumenal world and not of a divine intelligence, a personification his skepticism will not allow. "Final Soliloquy of the Interior Paramour" never concludes that God *is* the imagination. The identity is offered as though it were merely a hypothesis, for it is what *we say* and not our affirmation of what *is*. There is, however, in this poem mention of a knowledge or an order that arranges the conjunctions of things and the order of occurrences as they are, that brings mind and world together in the intricate pattern that is individual experience. This order (or knowledge perhaps) or this unity (or whole) manifested in the unity of human experience is an idea of a primal source for the arrangement of everything. With an idea of this kind, Stevens seems to be groping toward a concept of the divine like that of primordial divinity in *Process and Reality*.[16]

"Viewed as primordial," Whitehead says of his concept of deity, "he is the unlimited conceptual realization of the absolute wealth of potentiality. In this aspect, he is not *before* all creation, but *with* all creation." And then he adds a statement toward which Stevens seems to be reaching: "He is the unconditioned actuality of conceptual feeling at the base of things; so that, by reason of this primordial actuality, there is an order in the relevance of eternal objects to the process of creation."[17] In "Final Soliloquy of the In-

[16] I do not intend to imply that Stevens had *Process and Reality* in mind or any other specific statement of idea. Whitehead's passage on p. 521 is quoted to bring out the implications of Stevens' obscure references to the idea of divinity.

[17] Joseph N. Riddel in *The Clairvoyant Eye* (Baton Rouge, La., 1965) also mentions a parallel here with Whitehead's idea of God as primordial. Mr. Riddel's book is a developmental study of great importance to the student of Stevens.

terior Paramour" Stevens indicates his sense of an inherent knowledge in the order of things that determines the meeting of self and reality in the way that it occurs:

> We feel the obscurity of an order, a whole,
> A knowledge, that which arranged the rendezvous.
>
> Within its vital boundary in the mind.

VIII

The Mind in Root

The whole life of imagination and knowledge comes from within, from the restlessness, eagerness, curiosity, and terror of the animal bent on hunting, feeding, and breeding.[1] Santayana

1

When making a comparison between the mind and the senses or thought and perception or reason and intuition, Stevens usually puts his final trust in sentience. He is governed by the inherent bias of the poet for the body's faith in the palpable certainty of the world of immediate experience.

In spite of his idea that the world is revealed only in an individual version, that it is always, as he knows it, an invented world, nevertheless, he shares the responsive intuitive confidence of the poet in the reality of his immediate experiences and the trust that, as the world appears, so it is. In "A Collect of Philosophy" Stevens quotes from some notes sent him by Jean Paulhan that define the nature of the poet's concept of the world:

[1] *Scepticism*, p. 185.

"The first word of the philosophy of the sciences, today, is that science has no value except its effectiveness and that nothing, absolutely nothing, constitutes an assurance that the external world resembles the idea that we form of it. Is that a poetic idea? Antipoetic, rather, in that it is opposite to the confidence which the poet, by nature, reposes, and invites us to repose, in the world."[2]

Stevens, too, considers that confidence in the certitude of the world that is perceived immediately and daily is in the main tradition of poetry and that to know a reality beyond himself the poet has only to see and hear and in every way to engage in experience that he assumes is received just as given. And he is also aware of the tradition of speculative inquiry. In his view of this other tradition, a stance of inquiry is taken at a remove from immediate experience and, from this remove—the remove of theory—the familiar world of daily appearance vanishes.

As for his own poetry, everywhere the confidence of the poet in the world of appearance meets the speculation of the skeptic, for when he hypothesizes, "It is possible that to seem—it is to be," with this doubting "it is possible," certainty vanishes from experience. In his intrinsic bodily existence he walks confidently through the world; in his rational temper, he suspects that "his route lies through an image in his mind." The confidence of the poet in the world is also an acceptance of appearance as sign of reality, reliance on the immense fact of physical existence, insight into his own irrational nature, and recognition of the irrational force of events. The poet is intent on his engagement in the moment of present experience.

The supplemental opposites, physical life and cognition, represent two ways of knowing the world, and a number of

Stevens' poems express the theme that the world is truly realized in the life of the body and that abstract thought is itself a separation, a removal from the reality it considers. The position suggests a basic concept of *The World as Will and Idea*. In a passage that summarizes his idea of the fundamental disparity between direct physical contact with the world through the body and knowledge of the world, Schopenhauer explains that the intelligence that attempts to reach the world as an idea is thereby separated from the physical reality of that world. It is like a man who attempts to know a building from the outside, who walks around it, but can never enter, and, therefore, must content himself with mere names and images for the reality of rooms and the life within them:

> Thus we see already that we can never arrive at the real nature of things from without. However much we investigate, we can never reach anything but images and names. We are like a man who goes round a castle seeking in vain for an entrance, and sometimes sketching the facades.[3]

The predicament of the man who goes round a castle resembles that of the skeptic in "Palace of the Babies," who walks outside a structure of thought or faith which he never enters because of his disbelief:

> The disbeliever walked the moonlit place,
> Outside of gates of hammered serafin,
> Observing the moon-blotches on the walls.

Schopenhauer goes on to say that if one who investigates the nature of the world were a pure knowing subject, "a winged cherub without a body," he could never find the real world. Stevens' skeptic imagines that the palace holds, as pure know-

---

[3] *Will and Idea*, p. 115.

ing subjects, babies, perhaps cherubs,[4] with their dreams of fledgling wings or potential imaginative flights:

> If in a shimmering room the babies came,
> Drawn close by dreams of fledgling wing,
> It was because night nursed them in its fold.

The primal source of experience, creative night, he thinks, may nurse these pure knowing subjects that he imagines within the rooms; but, as for the disbeliever, the skeptic, "night nursed not him," and his skepticism separates him from the belief that he desires. The confusion of wings within his own mind is a confusion of thought. He pulls his hat down over his eyes as one who cannot see, "and in his heart his disbelief lay cold."

Another disbeliever is "The Dove in Spring," whose isolation is that of selfhood and who is a disbeliever in knowledge except that of his own living being. The subjective creature, in its insecurity "like a man / Who keeps seeking out his identity," is depicted as a bird within its imagined cage, the dove, the brooder howling its uncertainty, its doubt of that which is beyond the confines of its own nature. And in the intense littleness of its subjectivity, that tiny point at the center of circumstance, and in the darkness of its physical interior, the self, the dove broods on its uncertainty:

> Brooder, brooder, deep within its walls—
> A small howling of the dove
> Makes something of the little there,
>
> The little and the dark, and that
> In which it is and that in which
> It is established. . . .

[4] The image of the pure knowing subject as a cherub is used by Santayana, but in his figure the cherubs are ideas: "Why should any wish or idea arise at all here and now? Is the mid-void peopled with them, as with little winged heads of cherubs, without bodies and without support?" *Realms of Being*, p. 313.

Like the dove secluded in the cage of its little establishment, its arrangements of order and reason, "like slits across a space," the thinking self in Stevens' poetry is often set apart from the world in an interior, a cavern or a room. In "The Bagatelles the Madrigals" the serpent, traditional symbol of knowledge, lies with eyes shut in a crevice of earth, for all people are secluded in a crevice of earth (meaning the body, that piece of earth); there they think, baffled by the countless random details, the irrational disorder of existence:

> And where is it, you, people,
> Where is it that you think, baffled
> By the trash of life,
> Through winter's meditative light?

In its interior of subjectivity and thought, the self turns from action to analysis, from the naked touch of intuition to the shadow world of idea. The skeptic, in his seclusion from actuality, is like the man in "Of the Surface of Things," unable to realize the world when enclosed by the walls of a room. When he emerges from his walk (the truth, Stevens says elsewhere, may depend on a walk around a lake), he discovers the world in the scene of his life and finds that it consists of three or four hills and a cloud or of whatever else is simply there.

"Extracts from Addresses to the Academy of Fine Ideas" opens with the opposition between concept and percept; here a sense of physical presence is given in subconscious perception. Only in an impossible Eden of corporeal immediacy—"a land beyond the mind"—could there be the naked life of unthinking direct experience. The world of daily conception that men share is an abstraction, created out of language and become a paper world rather than a sensory one. Compare percept and concept, he says in the opening of "Extracts from Addresses to the Academy of Fine Ideas":

> . . . Compare the silent rose of the sun
> And rain, the blood-rose living in its smell,
> With this paper, this dust. That states the point.

The paper flower and the garden of the Eden of truth occur with a similar though slightly different context of thought in Santayana's "Realm of Truth." Speaking of the usurpation of truth by convention, Santayana maintains that man deceives himself by substituting verbal conventions—precepts, conventional scientific or religious discourse—for "the material movement of things": "and the poor human soul walks in a dream through the paradise of truth, as a child might run blindly through a smiling garden, hugging a paper flower."[5]

Where, Stevens' poem asks, is the true world behind the paper world? Where can be found a lifetime of summer, the instant of the meeting of reality and mind in the glitter of experience? Only in an impossible covert like that of Eden can man in the nakedness of direct experience live a life of responsiveness, free of the unreality and the intervention of knowledge:

> Where is that summer warm enough to walk
> Among the lascivious poisons, clean of them,
> And in what covert may we, naked, be
> Beyond the knowledge of nakedness, as part
> Of reality, beyond the knowledge of what
> Is real, part of a land beyond the mind?

These several views of the validity of knowledge and experience are illustrated by Stevens' three poems on the dove. The skeptical speculative view is expressed in the anxiety of "The Dove in Spring." To counter the doubt of the reality of experience of the world, there is, deep within the physical being of man, "The Dove in the Belly," a self rapt by the con-

[5] *Ibid.*, p. 464.

tinual, manifest showing of things. Faith in the real presence of the world and belief in the verity of perception enable the self that is only a creature to feel the security of a nest in each moment that it trusts will be repeated in the next. Here is founded the strength and courage of the creature who trusts that the world from moment to moment is a totality of existence. Stevens describes this trust and acceptance of the world in "Song of Fixed Accord":

> Rou-cou spoke the dove,
> Like the sooth lord of sorrow,
> Of sooth love and sorrow,
> And a hail-bow, hail-bow,
> To this morrow.

Greeting each instant, each hour, as the whole of reality, the helpless animal self in this poem accepts that hour as changeless even though change and process go on within—change, the true lord of love and sorrow and the creator of all experience. There is no howling here like that of the skeptical dove ("The Dove in Spring"), for this is a song of perfect confidence in the presence of the world. The reality or "ordinariness" of each hour of its life is represented by the sun of that time, a stability of the present instant in a set succession of hours and a heaven of security within the nest of the present:

> The sun of five, the sun of six,
> Their ordinariness,
> And the ordinariness of seven,
> Which she accepted,
> Like a fixed heaven. . . .

2

The notion that to know is merely to regard one's own idea, that knowledge about is a poor substitute for an experience of, that an idea is always and inherently fictive permeates all of the poetry of Stevens. In "Esthétique du Mal," IV, the poet regards the dependence of living body on knowing mind as the inherent human flaw from which "fault / Falls out on everything." The concluding lines assert that the genius of the body, its ruling capacity for physical sentience, is wasted in the effort to know:

> The genius of the body, which is our world,
> Spent in the false engagements of the mind.

Stevens' skeptical view of reason is reinforced by his naturalism. Right or wrong, to speculate is the nature of the conscious self. Stevens finds idea an expression of the self and sees concept as made by an identity that is a thinking body. The reality of physical being, therefore, is always a particular reality of one singular person. Like Schopenhauer in the famous chapter on "The Objectification of the Will," Stevens usually implies that he is an individual only through his identity with his body and that when he attributes reality to the world, he must give it the reality that each of us finds in his own body. Perception of anything, of "A Dish of Peaches in Russia," is an engagement of the body with the world. And the body is also one with the self and all its history of affections, its identity spilled out in its individuality of memory merged with the present personal consciousness: "With my whole body I taste these peaches," the poem begins and then asks, "Who speaks?" The answer comes from a body and its whole history: "it must be that I, / That animal," whose engagement with experience is that of the real animal engaging in ferocities of sensory life. Each one, according to "Esthétique du Mal," has the necessity of being himself, "the unalterable necessity of being this unalterable animal."

The body as an irrational animal is an archetype. "Poetry Is a Destructive Force" uses this image to show the whole man composed of a body and its dormant emotions bearing the wakeful consciousness that is the rational man. These dormant emotions are sleeping beasts, and the reason lives within this animality:

> He is like a man
> In the body of a violent beast.

And according to "From the Misery of Don Joost," "my body, the old animal," is the intrinsic self of a lifetime composed of the storm and violence of its struggle with reality, its combat with the sun. Usually Stevens regards the vital animal nature of man as an immediate point of contact with the real world; the human animal participates in the physical life of the world, while the rational cognitive self must be content with the merely descriptive character of knowledge. In "The Latest Freed Man," he is, he says, "tired of the old descriptions of the world," and freeing himself from the need to find some kind of rational truth, he turns to his life of physical experience and becomes, as the poem's title has it, "The Latest Freed Man." The poem depicts a man sitting on the edge of his bed, just awake or conscious. He is, therefore, close to the unreasoning life of the senses. With its abundance of pure sentience, his consciousness is filled with the spontaneous intuition of the animal so that he sees "everything bulging and blazing and big in itself." Intent then on his immediate life, he becomes a vital natural creature flooded with the light of the sun that both creates and represents the actuality of his animal experience. "To be without a description of to be" is to turn from analysis of the world to the presence of the world. With the release of consciousness from abstraction, the self awakens to the simple physical reality of things; then the man is transformed from a speculating creature to a corporeal one, with the rational deliberation of the ant (Aesop's or La Fontaine's), turned in that instant of change into the strength and immensity, the mind-filling reality of being, symbolized by the organic life of the ox:

> To have the ant of the self changed to an ox
> With its organic boomings, to be changed
> From a doctor into an ox, before standing up,
> To know that the change and that the ox-like struggle
> Come from the strength that is the strength of the sun,
> Whether it comes directly or from the sun.

The mind is rooted within the body, and the body has the inherent faintness of the self described in the title of the poem "A Weak Mind in the Mountains." The botched fate that conjoins man's creativity with his mortal body is signified by the butcher's hand and the blood that spills:

> There was the butcher's hand.
> He squeezed it and the blood
> Spurted from between the fingers
> And fell to the floor.
> And then the body fell.

The poem characterizes the creative element of process as the green wind and the decreative element as the black wind; these two elements in the flux, in each instant simultaneously creating and destroying, whirl together upon the body. Depicting the continual defeat of the physical self, the faintness of physical being in the midst of the forces of change, the mind's blood falls; and the self, defeated by process, sleeps. The word *sleep* here has an open meaning that extends from the literal to the symbolic, from faintness and death to the sleep of inanimate things. The defenseless mind must die with its body, but there is a will to overcome its vulnerability. "Yet there was a man within me," the poem asserts of the mind's will to live, to transcend the body's weakness, to be one who might break the winds of process and rise above the earth. There is a kind of pathos implied in the impotency of the mind that imagines within it a power that is no more than a desire. To fulfill its desire, the self would have to become a pure knowing subject, for only a disembodied spirit "could have risen to the clouds," "could have stood up sharply in the sky."

To gain the impersonal view of man's fate that freedom from a perishing body alone can give, a late poem of Stevens, "One of the Inhabitants of the West," predicates an impossible pure being, "a reader without a body," the archangel of evening. The archangel addresses men as grossly physical, locked in the eternal form (eternally repeated) that Medusa or earth has put upon them, and says,

> "These are not banlieus
> Lacking men of stone,
> In a well-rosed two-light
> Of their own."

The scenes of life are not evil places (banlieus), the archangel says, devoid of men locked in the eternal form of man. The "well-rosed two-light" of the stanza is an image of the two elements of consciousness—perception and conception. Schopenhauer in the chapter on "The Objectification of the Will" uses this image of the two lights of perception and conception. To exist, man must, he says, "be lighted by a double knowledge; a higher power, as it were, of perceptive knowledge must be given him, and also reason, as the faculty of framing abstract conceptions."[6]

In the poem the archangel observes the evening star and praises "this one star's blaze." The archangel sees it first as the pure impersonal light of evening. Then, taking a cue

---

[6] *Will and Idea*, p. 167.

from the archetypal image of consciousness as a blaze of light, he submits it as symbolic of man's consciousness, which is necessarily incarnate and, therefore, analogous to a drop of blood rather than a point of light:

> "Suppose it was a drop of blood . . .
> So much guilt lies buried
> Beneath the innocence
> Of autumn days."

Human consciousness is always embodied, always blooded, and all of the blood of man can be reduced to the tiny point of his subjectivity. It is only a drop in the vast account of universal process. Just so much, just that much guilt—that of making man not only suffer death but also be conscious of his death—is the guilt that lies buried in the past (the autumn days); only man with his self-awareness must endure his death in conception. The innocence of autumn of the poem is the innocence of nature that is so often in Stevens the innocence of unconsciousness and lack of intent.

Stevens' angels seem to be fairly close to Rilke's in that they are personations of idealized perfected mind. The archangel of evening is higher understanding, but the angel of reality in "Angel Surrounded by Paysans" is a personification of an intuition of reality "cleared of its stiff and stubborn man-made set." Intuition of this kind is the element in human experience that is the glimpse, the sense a man has that the world is truly there and has its own presence and existence other than his. The angel of reality is, according to the title of the poem, "surrounded by paysans." The paysans represent humanity, and when the angel says that he is one of them (men), he explains that "being one of you / Is being and knowing what I am and know." Intuition, one can then infer, is essentially human and rooted in the body; for the word *paysans,* the countrymen to whom the angel relates himself, holds connotations of the earthly or physical. The fugitive nature of the angel of reality is that of the otherness, the noumenal essence of the real. Intuition of reality is the necessary angel because only through intuition is the world glimpsed. Intuition gives the feel of the actual to experience, the sense of something known that is separate and distinct.

Basically, Stevens has an implicit confidence in the physical presence of the world as the very circumstance of existence. In spite of the idea of the invented world, a physical presence is assumed for any object that looms in experience, for intuition of mass and emplacement is the basis of awareness of an object. In "Saint John and the Back-Ache," a sense of the presence of something is held to be antecedent to the recognition of that thing. And physical presence itself is evidence of the reality of a thing:

> . . . The world is presence and not force.
> Presence is not mind.

The notion of actual presence in this poem is the sense of physical reality that is native to animal awareness. Husserl speaks of simple awareness of the world of things, a physical world surrounding the ego and immediately open to intuition: "I am aware of a world, spread out in space endlessly, and in time becoming and become, without end." Husserl remarks that a sense of presence is an *a priori* that does not need conscious attention: "corporeal things somehow spatially distributed are *for me simply there,* in verbal or figurative sense 'present,' whether or not I pay them special attention. . . ."[7] Stevens' poem also suggests that the physical being of the actual prevails in the mind before any conception of it can form: "It fills the being before the mind can think." The poem also contains a hint of Santayana's idea of non-sensuous apprehension, his conjecture that, prior to

---

[7] *Ideas,* trans. W. R. Boyce Gibson (New York, 1962), p. 91.

instant perception of something real and identification of it for use (or inattention), a presence is immanent in animal watchfulness, "as I turn my head to see who is there, before I see who it is."[8]

The Saint John of the poem suggests that the presence of something enters awareness as part of the continual upwelling of experience and is an unforeseen event like all the indeterminable changes and occurrences of the flux. Therefore, to describe emerging awareness of presence, the instant revelation of a thing is expressed by illustrations of spontaneous natural change: a sudden show of color in the sea or the moment of the shift from summer to fall. But Saint John, the personified intelligence and the apostle of the word, finds that his account of presence is only a statement of what it is not. His illustrations are neither intuitions (angels) nor brilliant guesses at the nature of reality—not even the fortune of the player with his guitar whose individual sense of the world is his sole gamble for reality:

> These illustrations are neither angels, no,
> Nor brilliant blows, thereof, ti-rill-a-roo,
> Nor all one's luck at once in a play of strings.

A sense of the immanence of things is subliminal, rising from a source even below that of the feeling of poetry: "I speak below / The tension of the lyre." With exquisite drollery, the saint argues that presence is the basic mystery of the existence of things and that the self uses its groping imagery to confront the distance between its subjectivity and the objectivity of the world:

> They help us face the dumbfoundering abyss
> Between us and the object. . . .

"The dumbfoundering abyss" or space between subject and object is a common philosophic metaphor that compares the

[8] *Scepticism*, p. 179.

difference between subjective knowing and the object of knowing to a spatial separation. The difference or distance between subject and object is the essential condition of all cognition, the vantage from which anything is perceived, in fact, the basis of conscious life: "The little ignorance that is everything."

Jung has written a passage that illuminates this idea of Stevens that the separateness of the subject of knowing from the unknown physical world creates the essential condition of the subject-object relationship:

> The self, regarded as the Counter-pole of the world, its "absolutely other," is the *sine qua non* of all empirical knowledge and consciousness of subject and object. Only because of this psychic "otherness" is consciousness possible at all. Identity does not make consciousness possible; it is only separation, detachment, and agonizing confrontation through opposition that produce consciousness and insight.[9]

One poem (XIX of "The Man with the Blue Guitar") repeats this theme in a version that shows the self detaching itself from nature to confront it as one of its voices. Stevens wrote a note on this poem for his translator, Renato Poggioli, who quotes it in the postcript of *Mattino Domenicale ed Altre Poesie:* " 'I want to be the lion in the lute,' " Stevens says, " 'and then, when I am, I want to face my parent and be his true poet. I want to face nature the way two lions face one another—the lion in the lute facing the lion locked in stone.' "[10] In this poem, the consciousness is a part of nature, a monster, too, a lion in a lute like the lion in stone that it faces. In this confrontation, the self is only another form of nature; even its expression of the reality it faces, its poetry, is part of the activity of the natural world: "I want to be

[9] *Psyche and Symbol*, p. 136.
[10] P. 179.

nature in the form of a man, with all the resources of nature," Stevens says. The poet, rooted in the world and yet standing before it as its intelligence, becomes, in his expression of his sense of it, the orphic instrument of nature fulfilling its natural function of realization by

> Being the lion in the lute
> Before the lion locked in stone.

The lion in the lute confronting the lion in stone is one of Stevens' many images of the mind regarding reality. In some versions this confrontation may seem to be an opposition, as in the oft-quoted phrase from "The Noble Rider": "a violence from within that protects us from a violence without." An important aspect of this apparent duality is that it is essentially a unity, for both elements (mind and reality) are lions, both are violences, and the force of mind seems to be only one of the forces of nature. The poet, recognizing this unity of the two violences, the two monsters, wishes to be no more than "that in nature, which constitutes nature's very self." This phrase, as well as the rest of Stevens' note on the poem, expresses his inherent naturalism.

3

With the usual meaning of *sleep* and *wakefulness*, Stevens concurrently uses the terms figuratively to imply that consciousness is an awakening out of the universal sleep of matter. In his skeptical bent, he wonders if man's consciousness is a true wakefulness or only a restlessness of the sleep of things. Poem one of "Two Versions of the Same Poem" describes the self as "swollen / With thought, through which it cannot see," and asks if thought is no more than a fitfulness, as in dream perhaps:

>   . . . Does it
> Lie lengthwise like the cloud of sleep, not quite
> Reposed? . . .

To speak of consciousness as an awakening is to use an
archetypal figure that is, in a sense, a literal fact. The figure
is common in metaphysical discussions of the nature of
consciousness, like that of Santayana, who regards the organism in its life principle (the psyche, he calls it) as a mode
or condition of substance and says that "sleep is in a manner
the normal condition of the psyche." There is always a
potential in matter for life, Santayana feels, and he says that
"we may fancy that a sort of sub-soul or potential life sleeps,
and will always sleep, in the universe of matter, ready to
shape it, when opportunity occurs, into the likeness of all
essence."[11] Stevens, too, in a number of passages suggests that
there is a deep sleep of things (the non-conscious) and a
lighter sleep of man (the unconscious) and that man wakens
to light and action and perception, as in "The Red Fern":

>   . . . But wait
> Until sight wakens the sleepy eye
> And pierces the physical fix of things.

"The sleepy eye" is the infant self, the sleepy *I* (in Stevens'
recurrent pun), the undeveloped consciousness just wakening
to the forms of things. Man awakens when intuition pierces
mere appearance and gives the insight of a mature consciousness; for sight is also apperception, and the object seen is
comprehended in terms of a whole field of relationships and
preconceptions, in terms of a moment's history.

The imagery of sleeping and waking, like so much of
Stevens' recurrent imagery, is already at work in the early
poems—"Earthy Anecdote" and "Anecdote of the Prince of
Peacocks," for example. The speaker of the latter poem, the

---

[11] *Realms of Being*, p. 341.

I, regards himself as the rational, the conscious aspect of the self. It is in the light of his imagination that he meets Berserk, the irrational part of self, seemingly conscious ("Oh, sharp he was / As the sleepless") and apparently real; for he is red in the blue of the moonlight and sun-colored, too, "as if awake / In the midst of sleep." The rational one, confident that thought is an expression of reason and unaware of its involvement with the irrational, is reminded by Berserk of the traps he has set among dreams and thoughts. (Very often in Stevens the meaning of the word *dreaming* includes thinking.) The *I* of the poem, the rational part of self, then realizes that the mind ("the blue ground") is made perilous by the traps and blocks of the irrational.

Stevens' figurative notion of dream becomes clearer when compared with that of Schopenhauer. In a passage of *The World as Will and Idea*, Schopenhauer discusses the distinction between dream and conscious experience and concludes that the sequence of one event with another gives to life its thread of connection; this is the continuum of consciousness that makes living a sequential narrative. The sense of a progression in experience, he says, seems broken in dream; for waking life is not a continuation of dream life, and "the only sure criterion by which to distinguish them [dream and reality] is in fact the entirely empirical one of awaking."[12] Stevens illustrates the apparent discontinuity of dream and reality in the early poem "Anecdote of Canna," using the term *dream* to signify abstract thought, according to the usual figurative sense of the word for him. Thought never sleeps, the poem maintains, allowing the plain inference that thought only exists in consciousness:

> His thought sleeps not. Yet thought that wakes
> In sleep may never meet another thought
> Or thing. . . .

[12] P. 32.

Just as a dream is a thought that wakes in sleep, so is abstract thought a consciousness in the midst of the natural and environing unconsciousness of the world; and any thought is only something imagined, never permanent, vanishing before a new one and, therefore, never meeting another thought and certainly never a thing. "X, the mighty thought, the mighty man" of the poem, is the speculative thinker whose abstractions fill his capitol or intelligence and who meditates or dreams his universals, his huge canna:

> Huge are the canna in the dream of
> X, the mighty thought, the mighty man.
> They fill the terrace of his capitol.

There is a contrast implied between thought and perception; for, when day-light comes and X turns to immediate experience, he cannot identify the universals of his thought (his dreams) with the actual phenomena, the real daylight canna, and he stands uncertain before the discrepancy between abstract concepts and actual things.

The anecdote of the alternation from sleep to waking, from dream to reality, expresses more than a disparity of thought and sensory experience. It very subtly places concept beside percept in order to present, with some amusement, the bewildering variety of kinds of cognition and represents our life of thought and experience in the image of one who is half asleep or half awake and whose life and thought may be a dream or an awareness.

To sleep, to wake, to be absorbed in reflection, to be sunk in animal somnolence and automatic sentience, are alternating states of being that provide "variation in the range and intensity of our realized knowledge." The quotation is from Whitehead, and the following passage from *Process and Reality* clarifies and carries further the sense of diversity and disparity in our kinds of knowledge that Stevens' poem suggests:

We sleep; we are half-awake; we are aware of our perceptions, but are devoid of generalities in thought; we are vividly absorbed within a small region of abstract thought while oblivious to the world around; we are attending to our emotions—some torrent of passion—to them and to nothing else; we are morbidly discursive in the width of our attention; and finally we sink back into temporary obliviousness, sleeping or stunned.[13]

In "An Ordinary Evening in New Haven," IV, the men who resist illusion—"plain men in plain towns"—by their resistance restrict to the purely factual the range and variety of concept; dismissing the elaborations of the imagination, they want only the primitive, the perceptual range of consciousness. Man's consciousness, whether he will or not, is always "snuffed out," reduced to animal unconsciousness, and, he sinks back, in Whitehead's phrase, "sleeping or stunned":

> The plainness of plain things is savagery,
> As: the last plainness of a man who has fought
> Against illusion and was, in a great grinding
>
> Of growling teeth, and falls at night, snuffed out
> By these obese opiates of sleep. . . .

The plainness that rejects the life of the imagination is a savagery because it is close to animal reflexes and animal somnolence. But the animal nature of man, Stevens indicates, has an inherent need for the illusions that enable him to increase the range and variety of conceptual life, the fictions by which he may live, awake or conscious. The life of practical action finds its "diviner opposite" in the life of thought and art, in the whole range of the abstract or fictive.[14]

[13] P. 244.

[14] See the well-known passage that says the poet creates "the world to which we turn incessantly and without knowing it and that he gives to life the supreme fictions without which we are unable to conceive of it." *NA,* p. 31.

4

When Stevens depicts the self as an animal, it is usually with the life of action and feeling in mind. When he sees the self as vegetable, the image is used to describe human development as a growth in accordance with its natural organic destiny, with all the blooming of art, of thought, of the higher reaches of consciousness, rooted in matter or earth.[15] In Poem V of "An Ordinary Evening in New Haven," the self is a tree with its roots "held fast tenaciously in common earth" and its branches extending to the sky, there searching for "such majesty as it could find."

In another version of this traditional image of the organic nature of self, Lady Lowzen is a tree weaving her many arms, for which, as in the title of the poem, "Oak Leaves Are Hands." The vegetable imagery of the second section of "The Rock" depicts leaves as vision blooming into conception that covers the nothingness of the rock with the elaborations of leaves and flowers in a burgeoning of sentience:

> They bud the whitest eye, the pallidest sprout,
> New senses in the engenderings of sense,
> The desire to be at the end of distances,
>
> The body quickened and the mind in root.

By the evidence of many poems, it is obvious that Stevens assumed that there is a naturalistic basis for the life of the imagination and that poetry itself is a flowering of the natural world. Just as consciousness is a temporary waking from the sleep of the unconscious natural world, just as reason is the illusion of self-command of the irrational natural creature, just as the attempt to know reality and all the subtlety of

---

[15] Schopenhauer sees the knowing subject, the individual mind, rooted in the world: "But he is himself rooted in that world; he finds himself in it as an *individual*, that is to say, his knowledge, which is the necessary supporter of the whole world as idea, is yet always given through the medium of a body . . ." *Will and Idea*, p. 115.

thought is only the self-regard of nature, with reality looking into that mirror, the mind: "a glass / The sun steps into, regards and finds itself"—just as all these things are aspects of the natural world, so also the voice of poetry is only a sound like all the other real noises of things and voices. Poetry is a form of ordered meaning abstracted from the sound that words make. All intentional meaningful utterance is ultimately no more than sound, like the spontaneous cries of all the creatures of the world or like the accidental noises of things shaken or in motion: sound of wind, water, things in friction or impact. "The Region November" offers the notion that the sound of the movement of trees in wind is part of the wordless utterance that is the blind expressiveness of the unconscious world, an utterance without intent that is like a basis or beginning out of which evolve the sounds of meaning. In itself this inarticulate noise of things is

> . . . so much less than speech,

> Saying and saying, the way things say
> On the level of that which is not yet knowledge. . . .

This saying and saying without speech is like the search for the word in "To the Roaring Wind," the sound of things that have not wakened into consciousness and are, therefore, "in the distances of sleep." The roaring wind is searching for a syllable, for the very seed of a language. It is the universal search of will for the word—for meaning and consciousness. "The Search for Sound Free from Motion" implies that the word or the use of sound as language is a finding of such a search. Sound from mindless motion is signified by the turning of a gramophone, image of the turning earth, reiterating (parl-parling) all its sounds—sounds of weather, leaves, water—as one utterance, as its word:

> All afternoon the gramophone
> Parl-parled the West-Indian weather.

> The zebra leaves, the sea
> And it all spoke together.

The world repeats a sound from motion, and that sound is its word ("the world as word"), a sound compounded of the many voices of wind, typhoon, and the turning world suggested by the use in one stanza of the portmanteau word *gramaphoon*. But you—and the poet addresses man—you *used* the sound (the word), for the sound of speech is only one element of all the sounds of motion that speak together:

> The many-stanzaed sea, the leaves
> And it spoke all together.
> But you, you used the word,
> Your self its honor.

Sound or "the world as word" becomes, in the human use of it, a sound free from motion, a sound created by mind; and in mind the world lives and speaks, repeats its sound, but with conscious intent, with a selectivity that "balances / The syllable of a syllable."

Primarily, speech is an utterance and a manifestation of the mind's inner discourse with reality,[16] but it is a monologue without an answer, as indicated in the title of the poem "Continual Conversation with a Silent Man." The silent man as reality is personified in the title, is called in the poem "a turquoise monster moving round," and therefore is, according to Stevens' color symbolism, an imagined reality. Its (reality's) reply to the continual discourse of the flow of human thought is only the sound of the motion of things, of the monster's moving about:

> It is not a voice that is under the eaves.
> It is not speech, the sound we hear

[16] See Roy Harvey Pearce's "Wallace Stevens: The Last Lesson of the Master" in *The Act of the Mind* for another view of the mind's discourse with reality. Mr. Pearce also presents an interesting account of the tendency toward naturalism in Stevens and indicates the idea of the confrontation of mind and nature.

> In this conversation, but the sound
> Of things and their motion: the other man,
> A turquoise monster moving round.

That all sounds—the sound of things, the cry of life, and the utterance of man—are, after all, only elaborations of the same sound is the theme of Poem III of "Notes toward a Supreme Fiction." The Arabian who casts his stars about the room to predict the future is a personification of the speculative mind whose discourse is part of "life's nonsense" and is built upon the related nonsense of the cry of the dove and the noise of inanimate matter. Another poem from the same work reduces the meaning of man's discourse with reality to a cry of the self whose nature is to turn reality into personal experience: "Bethou me, said sparrow, to the crackled blade." All other sounds are the mindless or idiot sounds of natural phenomena, and beside them the utterance of the self, even its endless repetition of "bethou me," is an order, a harmony, a transcendence of the sounds of unconscious nature:

> There was such idiot minstrelsy in rain,
> So many clappers going without bells,
> That these bethous compose a heavenly gong.

Transcendence or not, it is still merely a sound in the flux, and like any other sound, the poem concludes, it will cease.

The word, like the noise of motion, the cry of the self, even the utterance of the poem that gives meaning to the world, is only another sound issuing from the ground of being; for poetry is one of "The Creations of Sound," according to the title of a poem that accounts for the feeling that words and meaning seem to come to the writer, the poet, as though "from the floor, rising in speech we do not speak." This is the spontaneous nature of language, and poetry itself issues from universal creativity, finding through the individuation of the poet the syllable of poetry:

> If the poetry of X was music,
> So that it came to him of its own,
> Without understanding, out of the wall

If poetry is music in the sense that it is an expression of primal will (like Schopenhauer's idea of music), the poet could be a man "too exactly himself," so much an individual separate being as to be no more than an obstruction for or adulterator of that sound. But man is truly a natural being, another piece of earth, his poetry only one sound among all the sounding of things. Silence or non-being is the basic condition: like air it lies all about, enveloping the individual sounds; and sound is like sediment or dirt, even the sound of poetry. For Stevens, as the poet of naturalism, it is not understanding that poetry increases; it is reality: "speech is not dirty silence / Clarified. It is silence made still dirtier."

Stevens maintains that poetry is a natural phenomenon, never a precious or separate activity. According to "An Ordinary Evening in New Haven," XII, it is not only an element of the actual, of something that happens in the universal flux; it is also a speech or cry for that particular occasion of which it is so truly a part and no more than a part:

> The poem is the cry of its occasion,
> Part of the res itself and not about it.

Santayana has a figure that defines the individuality of any moment as marked by the cry of its occasion. The individuality of a moment gives actuality to it, he says, and its uniqueness is celebrated by the particular sound and movement of that moment, its own leap and cry: "because that very leap and cry which brings each moment to birth cuts it off from everything else."[17] "The poem is the cry of its occasion" uses a compound of image and thought that is like

[17] *Realms of Being*, p. 254.

that of Santayana, for certainly a poem is the leap and sound of the individual moment of an experience of it. And, since nothing can be said to exist for any one person that is not a part of experience and because experience itself is only an element of the total flux, there is no category that separates poetry from other forms of existent reality.

Stevens' poetic meditation on appearance and reality, "Description without Place," concludes with his account of the part that language plays in the continual creation of appearance. The world, he says, is a "world of words." What is said or thought fixes the moment in the imagination and is a determinant of the way the next present moment seems; it portends the future by affecting the sense of things: "like rubies reddened by rubies reddening." This whole poem is clarified by a reading of Whitehead's chapter "Appearance and Reality," in *Adventures of Ideas*.[18] The line just quoted contains in essence Whitehead's idea of the immanence of the past in a present occasion and the immanence of the future in the past, for one experience of the world emerges out of another. Stevens assumes that so much of human experience is made up of language that the theory of the concept of the world through verbal description is a basic theory:

> It is the theory of the word for those
>
> For whom the word is the making of the world,
> The buzzing world and lisping firmament.
>
> It is a world of words to the end of it,
> In which nothing solid is its solid self.

In "An Ordinary Evening in New Haven," XXVIII, Stevens is the severe insistent master who would keep proving the theory of the nature of poetry to be also the theory of the nature of all life, for anything thought or written is an

[18] See especially p. 219.

actual occurrence, as actual as a conversation in a cafe or a memory of a city or an account of a trip or a picture postcard. Concurrent with any theory of human imaginings—with all longing for and grasping at what we conceive out of what we desire—there is the realization that a poem is an actual act of an actual self and a recognition

>   . . . that the theory
> Of poetry is the theory of life,
>
> As it is, in the intricate evasions of as,
> In things seen and unseen, created from nothingness,
> The heavens, the hells, the worlds, the longed-for lands.

Poetry for Stevens is above all a celebration of the existence of individual experience. In this respect also it is "the cry of its occasion." And, as a deed that is a realization of one actual person, it is thus part of the *res* or an element of all physical occurrence. The poem is part of the *res*, Stevens says, because the poem is a real expression of an actual person: "In all his poems," he concludes, "with all their enchantments for the poet himself, there is the final enchantment that they are true. The significance of the poetic act then is that it is evidence. It is instance and illustration. It is an illumination of a surface, the movement of a self in the rock."[19] The movement of a self in the rock is a restlessness like that of "one awake in the midst of sleep," the wakefulness of the consciousness. Stevens, like Crispin, never could forget that poetry is

> The wakefulness or meditating sleep,
> In which the sulky strophes willingly
> Bore up, in time, the somnolent deep songs.

The wakefulness of the consciousness receives poetry from the sleep of the unconscious. Its deep songs are somnolent because they arise from the universal sleep of nature.

[19] *OP,* p. 241.

IX

Sun, Moon, Day, Night, Music, and Rock

No longer in a merely physical universe, man lives in a symbolic universe.[1] Cassirer

1

In one of his aphorisms, Stevens speaks of "the image without meaning and the image as meaning," the word *meaning* here signifying symbolic import. For example, the word *night* is a possible symbol. "The heavy nights of drenching weather" illustrates a non-symbolic usage; and "the night / That lights and dims the stars," a symbolic usage. Stevens turns at will from the customary usage of a word to a usage that in itself demands interpretation. A response to that demand will take into consideration not only the figurative significance of the context but also the recurrence of the image in close association with certain statements of idea.

The thought in a poem of Stevens is composed of an interchange of statement and symbolic imagery. The image fills out the statement, carries the implication that can never be

[1] *An Essay on Man* (New Haven, 1962), p. 25.

adequately expressed in expository form. "Wild Ducks,
People and Distances," for example, opens with a statement
of one of Stevens' recurring notions—the idea that there is
no determinable object without a subject, that specific things
need specific experiences, and that the life of the world is
the life of a consciousness:

> The life of the world depends on that he is
> Alive, on that people are alive, on that
> There is village and village of them, without regard
> To that be-misted one and apart from her.

"That be-misted one" is nature personified as woman. Nature
as reality apart from human experience must be expressed
by a symbol; otherwise, it could not be expressed at all. She
is obscured or "be-misted," inconceivable, because only an
abstraction. Stevens' figurative representations of reality,
like the rock or the woman; or of the cycle of being, as in the
imagery of day and night or of the seasons; or of individual
experience, like the musician with his instrument and his
music, are an implicative language in themselves and supplement the accompanying statement of idea.

In the first section of "The Rock," the image of the rock,
like that of "that be-misted one" of the former poem, embodies the idea of the unrealized natural world. If unrealized,
it is like a nothingness and is without known existence. It
must be conceived as a possibility or as a will-to-be. It is
as though the possible has the desire to become actual in the
particular vision of an individual being:

> As if nothingness contained a métier,
> A vital assumption, an impermanence
> In its permanent cold, an illusion so desired
>
> That the green leaves came and covered the high rock....

The "métier," the "assumption," the "impermanence," the
"illusion"—all are terms to describe the individual subjective

life of the self; and the "nothingness," the "permanent cold," and the "high rock" are terms for the objectivity that enters light and life and existence only in an individual consciousness. As for the green leaves, these represent the living thoughts that grow in man's seasons and that cover the rock. In these experiences it is as though the ground of being attained its desire to be by means of the specific vision of an individual being.[2] The leaves and the blooms are examples of Stevens' frequent tree or floral or vegetation imagery to indicate that the creations of man's higher consciousness are a natural growth and to complement his symbolic use of the imagery of the seasons and of day and night.

Often Stevens uses the sun as an emblem of the fulfillment of the subject-object relationship. The image is that of reality realized, of the prime moment of experience in its continuing present. The sun of "Extracts from Addresses to the Academy of Fine Ideas" is an eye that continually regards the earth:

> . . . Sun is
> A monster-maker, an eye, only an eye,
> A shapener of shapes for only the eye. . . .

Many of Stevens' poems present the sun as realization of earth. In that realization, the earth, which is otherwise a "be-misted one" and a nothingness, becomes "the invented world." Then the subject is at one with the object, mind with experience, and by analogy, "the sun is the country wherever he is" ("Esthétique du Mal," VI).

The sun at noon implies the idea of a continuing present, and the rising sun and setting sun are seen from the viewpoint of an observer who is aware of process and of a coming and going in the flux of experience. In "The World as Meditation" the sun ("Is it Ulysses that approaches from

---

[2] Roy Harvey Pearce identifies the rock with the ground of being. See *The Continuity of American Poetry* (Princeton, 1961), p. 411.

the east, / The interminable adventurer") is always approaching Penelope, who, in her own person, is a part of earth and representative of the content of experience in the subject-object relationship.[3] Therefore, the sun is conceived from the point of view of oncoming experience. The sun "kept coming constantly so near" because the subject-object relationship is a separateness or distance between subject and object as well as a continual approach of subject toward object.

The sun is a symbol of being, and being is a realization as well as a reality. In the first poem of "Notes toward a Supreme Fiction" Stevens uses the image with a concurrent dual meaning; for the sun of this poem that exists in itself and whose existence has nothing to do with our embellishments, our names for it, must be "in the difficulty of what it is to be." By this description the sun is an instance of objective being, and by synecdoche it stands for the idea of the presence of the world. Since the world is also a human conception, the sun thus stands for both worlds, for the invented as well as the objective world, and that is Stevens' definition in imagery of the nature of being.

The symbolic import of the sun image pervades the imagery of day and night and the seasons. The sun that stands for the idea of objective being, by virtue of polarity, influences the import of Stevens' night imagery. Thus, night or darkness usually holds implications of non-being or pre-existence. The sun that exists always in its "consummate

[3] The poem is an example of Stevens' essentially ambiguous use of images: it is as if the sun were Ulysses and the earth were Penelope; yet, the two mythical characters retain their identity. Martz sees the figurative nature of the poem and reads it in terms of its human significance in "Wallace Stevens: The World as Meditation." The subject-object relationship also lies within the ambiguous field of reference of the poem as it does in so many of Stevens' later poems. It is the ultimate abstraction of the lover seeking the beloved, in this poem depicted from the point of view of the woman or of the longing of the object to be reached by the subject. In other poems lover desiring beloved may be abstracted as the mind seeking reality, with the mind as lover and reality as beloved.

prime" in "Esthétique du Mal," VI, at the same time is continually being devoured by night or non-being. Figuratively the poem depicts sun as present being losing bloom and fruit (phenomena). Night is an insatiable bird:

> . . . A big bird pecks at him
> For food. The big bird's bony appetite
> Is as insatiable as the sun's. . . .

The sun's appetite is creative and the bird's, decreative. Generally the poet associates being with day and non-being with night. The bird feeding on the sun suggests the darkness and the void that feeds on light and reality. The ambiguous nature of the sun symbol is shared by the night symbol; both represent man's interior world as well as his cosmic environment. In this additional sense sun is a consciousness continually creating experience, and the bird is man's inner darkness or subconsciousness feeding upon the rejected experiences, the blooms falling downward, "the yellow bloom of the yellow fruit / Dropped down from turquoise leaves."

The significance of the twin poems "The News and the Weather" depends upon a similar set of associations. The "news" of the first poem is the fresh appearance of things newly given in experience. The world of the sun is news because just seen, just become, and is always a newness like all appearance. The weather of the second poem is the sense of it all: the way the world seems in the feeling of it, the air, the weather that conditions each instant. In this poem the unconscious or interior creative dark is addressed as a tree, as a woman, as Solange, probably meaning by that name earth spirit.[4] The interior darkness as the unconscious is the

---

[4] "Solange" is the name by which he addresses this· creative unconsciousness. The word may be formed from *sol ange*: literally, soil or earth angel. It is a "nigger name," the poem says, and means by that a black name. Several critics, Northrop Frye, in "The Realistic Oriole," for one, notice the fact that Stevens uses *nigger* with a special non-racial significance.

nothingness out of which conscious experience emerges. It is man's black spirit: "A nigger tree and with a nigger name." Solange is a tree, like the self that Lady Lowzen represents, because the creative unconscious is rooted in the earth that is the body. The interior dark or blackness suggested by "nigger" is an aspect of the archetypal primal night, discussed later in this chapter.

The darkness of an unknown sea suggests the idea of non-being and pre-existence in "The Man with the Blue Guitar," XVIII, and the sunrise is compared to oncoming experience out of past experience:

> . . . as daylight comes,
>
> Like light in a mirroring of cliffs,
> Rising upward from a sea of ex.

The cycle of day very often represents figuratively the cycle of being. The zenith of the sun connotes the fullness of existence: noon is the culmination, the absolute vertical of both sun and being, "straight up, an élan without harrowing," with "straight up" describing the physical sun and the "élan without harrowing" suggesting that being is at its peak. The poem from which this line is quoted, "What We See Is What We Think," describes noon as the instant of full being, the division between becoming and disintegration:

> One imagined the violet trees but the trees stood green,
> At twelve, as green as ever they would be.
> The sky was blue beyond the vaultiest phrase.

The distinction between the living green and the first intrusion of deterioration, signified by the color of shadows, by violet and gray, is the distinction between creation and decreation:

> Twelve and the first gray second after, a kind
> Of violet gray, a green violet, a thread
> To weave a shadow's leg or sleeve. . . .

Thus, the symbolic cycle of day is divided into two halves, and the first half represents that aspect of the process of being Stevens calls the "yes" in "The Well Dressed Man with a Beard": "yes is this present sun." With afternoon, implications of the "no" begin, and the enactment of the "no" occurs when present forms become forms entering the past and, rejected by the process of change, lose being, slide over "the western cataract," with the sun declining into night. But because things exist, in the poetry of Stevens, in terms of the flux of experience, the nature of being is nearly always seen as an event of simultaneous emergence, fulfillment, and disappearance; for process involves the coming and going of experience in each instant.

Stevens regards the progression of the seasons and alternations of day and night as illustrations of his sense of things continually emerging and existing and falling and vanishing. In spring, he knows the incompleteness of things; he senses possibility, and being seems a continual becoming. In autumn "everything is half dead"; desolate air and empty perspective surround things in their passage; he senses dilapidation, anticipates disintegration. Winter is a nothingness and summer, the consummation of being, the instant of present reality. According to "The Motive for Metaphor" the nature of the self is such that it cannot endure a permanent present of absolute reality that the peak of summer represents, for the self can only live in mutation. The poem argues that the self enjoys the exhilaration of change implicit in beginnings, in all the unaccomplished growth of spring, and that the self also likes the pathos of change implicit in deterioration and in the decrepitude of autumn. But the self shrinks from any absolute present of fact. In Stevens' poem the flash of the present, which must be avoided in attention, is the moment of full and intolerable confrontation with reality:

> The weight of primary noon,
> The A B C of being . . .

The absolute present for Stevens (the peak of summer that is implied but never mentioned in this poem) is the present instant of full experience, when the self, composed as it is of thought and feeling, is in contact with the physical world and when, in the act of direct experience, matter touches mind in the tangent of "steel against intimation," of physical reality against pure subjectivity. It is also the fatal moment, the instant of continual dying that is each instant of experience.

"Credences of Summer" describes the peak of summer as the moment of perfection of the present toward which all becoming tends, the present moment with everything behind and nothing of actual time beyond, the self poised in existence, surrounded by its images of love and desire that consummate its moment of realized life:

> . . . these fathers standing round,
> These mothers touching, speaking, being near,
> These lovers waiting in the soft dry grass.

Another figure of this poem depicts the present as a summit of existence, and, when speaking of this peak of being, the poem describes it as a mountain. This is an image of the immense basis of physical reality supporting existence. On top of that mountain, looking from the tower of survey or the vantage point of the present, stands the sun in the figure of an old man. To indicate that he is not a real person but only an abstract symbol of the physical being of the world, that he does not scan experience, he is said to be one "who reads no book."

The sun or day is identified with the consciousness that composes a daytime life in "An Ordinary Evening in New Haven," XXIII. It is the half of one's existence that is made up of thought, "the bodiless half." With a life that is half-day, half-night, the night is like "a long inevitable sound" that absorbs into itself and cancels the variety of consciousness; it is a sound in which all the separate selves merge into the one unconsciousness of sleep except for the occurrence of dreams with furtive desires and half-thoughts that are "disembodiments" like those of day. The night of sleep is a herald of the universal night, out of which being emerges and into which it descends, in accordance with this day-night symbolism. The maternal sound and the woman in black cassimere of this poem refer to a personification of night as the universal mother, from whom being comes.

2

In the ancient figure of primal night, Stevens embodies his notion of the unknowable ground of being. "Green is the night and out of madness woven" (from "The Candle a Saint") implies that the ground of being is meaningless (mad) and fecund (green) with possibility. Among the indefinite people of this poem—the sleepers, who are probably the poets, and the astronomers, whose imaginative insight is part of the irrational nature of being, part of its madness—is the visionary, who sees the image of night in the form of the abstract goddess Nox. "Moving and being," Stevens calls her, having in mind perhaps the Aristotelian idea that in movement being emerges. She is also the essential shadow or the basis of form created from darkness. "The image at its source," the poem adds, to show that all shape, all imagery, emerges out of this archetype of being:

> The noble figure, the essential shadow,
>
> Moving and being, the image at its source,
> The abstract, the archaic queen. Green is the night.

There is also the personification of night as the parent in "Phosphor Reading by His Own Light" ("That elemental parent, the green night") and as the nocturnal inhuman author of "Credences of Summer," X, who meditates the characters that the actual life of summer and the present enact. Unpersonified, night in "The Man with the Blue Guitar," XXXII, is both an environing and interior void, a darkness and a space in which all being moves and exists, joyous and procreant with all that is new and possible but irrational and without meaning in the human sense:

> How should you walk in that space and know
> Nothing of the madness of space,
>
> Nothing of its jocular procreations?

A sense of blank abstraction behind appearance, an obscure or unknown sea, impending or encompassing cold, the image of the rock, even the force of the flux are versions of this same notion of a primal base of existence. The color black imparts this special significance to whatever it modifies. "Black water breaking into reality" is an image that represents actuality emerging out of the ground of being. This pervading idea of Stevens that associates latent being with darkness and present being with sunlight is also a characteristic figure of Santayana. In "The Realm of Matter" he writes that

> . . . a phase of latency, silent but deeply real, often connects the phases of activity. Sleep and night are not nothing: in them substance most certainly endures, and even gathers strength, or unfolds its hidden coils.[5]

The primal darkness assumes an existence and emerges out of black non-being as a white or silver form in the poet's imagery. *Argentine* is a favored word for the silver or

[5] *Realms of Being*, p. 227.

glitter of life. The early poem "The Silver Plough-Boy" describes a primal blackness ("A black figure dances in a black field") that attains existence by becoming visible, by wrapping itself in a silver sheet.[6] The span of life often is given by Stevens a gay, active quality: it is a holiday in reality, a bonfire in winter, a walk in the park, a festival.[7] Here a life is a dance down a furrow in back of the crazy or irrational plow that defines the present moment of being. The conclusion is a charade of age and death and the return to non-being:

> How soon the silver fades in the dust! How soon the black
>   figure slips from the wrinkled sheet!
> How softly the sheet falls to the ground!

The blackness of this poem is an ultimate as well as a primal blackness. In "The Jack-Rabbit" ultimate blackness is suggested by the buzzard and by the black man who warns the rabbit dancing on its world of sand bars. There is also the ultimate dark of "Valley Candle," the huge night converging its black beams upon a candle of being until the flux extinguishes that single life; then beams of the night converge upon the afterimage, memory and the effect of that life.

The tiny light of conception burning in universal night is the conscious part of self, and the rest is the subliminal, the unconscious, the black creative basis of mind that feeds the flame of conscious life. The consciousness, the flame, blazes with created or fictive conception ("his actual candle blazed with artifice" according to "A Quiet Normal Life"). The

[6] Jung refers to the alchemical image of "the *spiritus niger* who lies captive in the darkness of matter" and who "reverts to his original luminous state in the mystery of alchemical transmutation." *Psyche and Symbol,* p. 178.

[7] Santayana also sees consciousness as a gaiety: "In consciousness the psyche becomes festive, lyrical, rhetorical." *Realms of Being,* p. 349.

mind from which the flame of consciousness issues is itself a
part of the primal dark. In "Mud Master" the basis of self,
the stuff of the mind, is the blind procreant stuff out of which
all impending experience is made. The poem speaks of the
human mind as "blackest of pickanines" to imply that the
mind is a part, even if only a small or infant part, of primal
night. To define its import, the poem characterizes the mind
as muddy, for mud, like clay, is an archetype of the idea of
prime substance; for example, mud conceived thus recurs in
Poem IV of "Notes toward a Supreme Fiction," in which
Stevens says, "There was a muddy centre before we
breathed."

With this conception of the mind as *mind* (as functional,
not as mere physical brain), with the idea of mind as the
creative source of whatever experience impends, he addresses
it as black man in "Nudity in the Colonies." Each man, then,
carries within him a bit of the creative potential, the night
out of which experience emerges. "A Word with José
Rodríguez-Feo" inquires if "night is the nature of man's
interior world," and the last line of "Owl's Clover" expresses
the conclusion that night and the imagination are one.

3

Through their intricate system of connotations, Stevens'
symbols tend to form clusters of import. Just as sun and
day compose a figurative complex of meaning, moon and
night also are associated symbolically. If night is the primal
creative source of all, moon is the creative imagination.
Their creativity is spontaneous, irrational, independent of
conscious human will: "The moon was always free from
him, / As night was free from him." Night is the irrational
unmeaning ground of being; moon, the light within darkness, like an intelligence within the unconscious, a creative

light "whose shining is the intelligence of our sleep," as it is described in Part 2 of "Three Academic Pieces." It is the primal imagination of the natural creative source, independent of the individual human imagination yet within it and infusing it.

In "Effects of Analogy" Stevens says, "The poet is constantly concerned with two theories," two ideas of the nature of the imagination.[8] According to the first idea the poet "comes to feel that his imagination is not wholly his own but that it may be part of a much larger, much more potent imagination, which it is his affair to try to get at." This is the creative source often symbolized by the moon and is very similar to Coleridge's primary imagination. The other theory, like the secondary imagination of Coleridge, has to do with the poet's own heuristic and intuitive imagination: "The second theory relates to the imagination as a power within him to have such insights into reality as will make it possible for him to be sufficient as a poet in the very center of consciousness."[9]

The distinction can be seen in Part 2 of "Three Academic Pieces," the essay-poem in *The Necessary Angel*. The moon here stands for the imagination of the first theory, and the word *imagination* itself stands for that of the second theory; this individual imagination is the "someone" of the title of the poem, "Someone Puts a Pineapple Together." The poem sets up pairings of sun and day, night and moon, human

[8] Obviously, Stevens is using Coleridge's idea of the primary and secondary imagination. "The primary Imagination I hold to be the living power and prime agent of all human perception, and as a repetition in the finite mind of the eternal act of creation in the infinite I AM. The secondary Imagination I consider as an echo of the former, co-existing with the conscious will, yet still as identical with the primary in the *kind* of its agency, and differing only in *degree*, and in the *mode* of its operation." *Biographia Literaria*, ed. John Calvin Metcalf (New York, 1926), p. 190. O'Connor, in *The Shaping Spirit*, first indicated Coleridge as a source for Stevens' idea of the imagination.

[9] *NA*, p. 115.

imagination and man, and creates out of them a sort of Hegelian formula: a thesis, antithesis, synthesis; in the synthesis occurs the sequence of consciousness or man's "endless effigies":

> It is as if there were three planets: the sun,
> The moon and the imagination, or, say,
>
> Day, night and man and his endless effigies.

In a number of poems, the moon is only the moon itself. The ordinary non-symbolic use of the word is sometimes confusing because of the dominant and, therefore, expected symbolic usage. The import of the symbol is never fixed and is always modified by the context in which it occurs. In "An Ordinary Evening in New Haven," XIX, the moon represents the imagination that colors our personal apprehension of the world at a given time. It is a light that rises in the mind, and under its influence everything is seen as it is felt. This is the imagination that is the sense of the world for us and the dominant mood of the moment. Another figurative usage suggests the idea that our imaginings are given rather than self-conceived. Thus, the moon can represent for the poet the upwelling of feeling, imagery, language that a poet of a different age might have called "inspiration."

In one poem Stevens identifies the moon with the poet's archetypal singing bird and, like Keats or Shelley or Arnold, addresses his bird as though it were an embodiment of the idea of the outpouring of poetry. With a just sense of the ambiguity of the symbol, it is both imagined bird and real moon, and the conjunction of the two composes the idea of the creative source of poetry. The poem is a celebration of the moment of life transformed into song, and the feeling of the moment is expressed lightly in its title, "God Is Good. It Is a Beautiful Night."

Look round, brown moon, brown bird, as you rise to fly,
Look round at the head and zither
On the ground.

Look round you as you start to rise, brown moon,
At the book and shoe, the rotted rose
At the door.

This was the place to which you came last night,
Flew close to, flew to without rising away.
Now, again,

In your light, the head is speaking. It reads the book.
It becomes the scholar again, seeking celestial
Rendezvous,

Picking thin music on the rustiest string,
Squeezing the reddest fragrance from the stump
Of summer.

The venerable song falls from your fiery wings.
The song of the great space of your age pierces
The fresh night.

The head and zither of the poet are seen as from above and from there dwindle into objects. The door, the book, the shoe, and the rotted rose are other aspects of the view from above and hold possible symbolic value. It is in the light of the moon of the creative imagination that the head is speaking, that it reads from its book and sings its song, turning the poetry of life and experience into the poetry of language. The string he plucks is the rustiest string because this poem, this song of his, is being sung at the present or latest moment and, therefore, is played on the oldest instrument—the ancient instrument of all poets before him.

In the last stanza the moon, his bird, is also the true moon, and like song, its light falls through the great space of its distance and of its age, suffusing him with a sense of the eternal processes, the vast repetitions of nature. But the song is also

truly his own song, the song of a poet celebrating his wonder
at the place where he finds himself at this moment. The
poet sings of a bird or a moon that is the self-same moon for
any of the succession of men or poets standing below in its
light, a moon that with its imagined fiery wings will rise, the
eternal phoenix again, each night for each poet.

4

In several accounts of universal motion and change,
Stevens variously describes the "sound" of the flux. It is like
the sound of friction, "a grinding going round" or "the
grinding ric-rac," and in "How to Live. What to Do" it is
the sound of the wind, "heroic sound / Joyous and jubilant
and sure." The sound is a vanishing music in "The Man
with the Blue Guitar," XXVI:

> A mountainous music always seemed
> To be falling and to be passing away.

The manifestation of the primal energy of process as
sound—sound of motion, sound of wind, sound of water,
sound of music—bears a resemblance to Schopenhauer's
famous analogy in *The World as Will and Idea* of music as
the principle of will in all things ("the in-itself of all phenomena, the will itself").[10] The link with Schopenhauer dis-
closes itself in "An Ordinary Evening in New Haven," XXI,
in which the sound becomes a musical form, the romanza,
and the idea of universal will as in Schopenhauer is presented
as the causal energy of existence—in Stevens' words "the will
of necessity, the will of wills":

> Romanza out of the black shepherd's isle,
> Like the constant sound of the water of the sea
> In the hearing of the shepherd and his black forms. . . .

[10] P. 272.

Once Stevens' symbolic use of *black* and of *music* is grasped, the black shepherd can be seen as an orphic figure representing the primal creative base, the darkness out of which being emerges. He is a symbolic figure resembling Nox in "The Candle a Saint," and his romanza is the music of universal creative will.

The poem mentions two islands, that of the black shepherd and the island of individual consciousness:

> Close to the senses there lies another isle
> And there the senses give and nothing take. . . .

The black shepherd's isle is the universal creative source, and its romanza, its music, is the latency of experience emerging from the dark creative source of being. The other isle symbolizes the reflection of the world composed by sentience within each mind. A quotation in Vaihinger's *The Philosophy of 'As If'* concerning the import of this image in eighteenth century stories of shipwreck like *Robinson Crusoe* shows the common association of the island image with the idea of conception:

> . . . the isolated basis of abstract and inwardly reflected thought is schematically clothed in the picture of a desert island in an immense ocean . . .[11]

The poem characterizes the other island as the isolation at the center of the self that is, "the opposite of Cythère"; for conception, unlike the love that joins one with another, is a solitary and individual expression of the self and its single will:

> The opposite of Cythère, an isolation
> At the centre, the object of the will, this place,
> The things around—the alternate romanza

The romanza out of the black shepherd's isle is that of uncreated, nonexistent and impending forms and events, and

[11] P. 192.

the alternate romanza is that of the appearance of reality to the self. The two romanzas, the two voices, "are a single voice in the boo-ha of the wind," the poem concludes; for in the nonsense, the irrational sound of the eternal flux, the individual will is lost in the voice of universal will.

Music, in Stevens' figurative use of it, may represent the primal energy or will, but it may also stand for a personal experience of the world. It is one will insofar as he conceives of a universal unrealized base for reality; it is many wills of the world if conceived as realized separately in many individuals. "Continual Conversation with a Silent Man" speaks of the tumult of separate wills that realize the world each in its individual way along with the universal will that is their creative source: "the never-ending storm of will, / One will and many wills." The flux of reality, with its many versions within individual thoughts, is "the wind, / Of many meanings in the leaves," for leaves are thoughts in Stevens' frequent use of vegetal imagery.

In "Thunder by the Musician" the tumult of will is manifested as music and is a storm of wills out of which emerges the individual will, holding aloft its consciousness. The creative source of things is also their destroyer; thus, the musician or source of being is not only a composer but also a butcher.[12] The poem is a depiction of the triumph of individual being in each moment with this violent personal will-to-be emerging out of the confusion of many possible forms of being. The thunder by the musician is the music of universal creative will:

> Sure enough, moving, the thunder became men,
> Ten thousand, men hewn and tumbling,
> Mobs of ten thousand, clashing together,
> This way and that.

[12] Creator is also butcher in "Ghosts as Cocoons."

> Slowly, one man, savager than the rest,
> Rose up, tallest, in the black sun,
> Stood up straight in the air, struck off
> The clutch of the others.

The subjective being or self, one of the mobs of possible thousands, is this will-to-achieve-being that rises up in a black sun; black is the color of the primal base of being, and the image of the black sun symbolizes an impending reality. This individual will is strong in its intense personal actuality and tallest in the dominant present of its own single life. Its individual identity strikes off the clutch of others who try to hold it to them and deny that identity. By its violent subjectivity, it alone holds aloft the diamond, the one thing that is precious.[13] The flashing egg-diamond is also a version of Stevens' image of the essence of a life as a flashing or glittering. And individual consciousness seems a unique possession to any self looking from its peak of subjective life, for it alone holds "the moment of light"; it is apex and height of life and peak of surveillance of all experience. There the self holds its individuality, according to the musician, the composer of events:

> And, according to the composer, this butcher,
> Held in his hand the suave egg-diamond
> That had flashed (like vicious music that ends
> In transparent accords).

The poet then considers his theme. It would have been better, he says, conceiving of the time in detachment, for the self to have been holding—what? In view of the indeterminable character of subjective being, he is unable to say what could have been better or even what it is that the self is holding. Even though the self expresses the violence of a will to live, though it shouts its self-assertion, the arm thrust

[13] In Oriental texts diamond is a symbol of individuation accomplished. See Jung and Kerényi's *Essays on Mythology*, p. 17.

up is trembling. It is weak with the faintness of the passage
of life. The welter of existence mixes the cries of the dead
and the speech of the living, and the sky is full of bodies.
This is the never-ending storm of will—the will to achieve
individual being. The poem concludes that it might be
better for a self (symbolized by its hands) to remain on a
level of mere blind activity without achieving the diamond
that stands for the height of consciousness, for self-awareness:

> It would have been better for his hands
> To be convulsed, to have remained the hands
> Of one wilder than the rest (like music blunted,
> Yet the sound of that).

The conflict out of which an individual being emerges
into its height of consciousness is compared to "vicious music
that ends / In transparent accords"; the lower grade of being
lacking conscious will, to "music blunted / Yet the sound
of that." Thus, in this poem Stevens associates both will and
music with the irrational contradictions of being and the
struggle to assert the individual self. Schopenhauer also finds
the conflicts of musical elements analogous to the conflicts
of individual wills that are a manifestation of universal will:

> . . . there yet remains an unceasing conflict between those
> phenomena as individuals, which is visible at every grade,
> and makes the world a constant battlefield of all those
> manifestations of one and the same will, whose inner con-
> tradiction with itself becomes visible through it. In music
> also there is something corresponding to this.[14]

There is the personal will of an individual and all its
details of momentary appetency summed up in its will-to-be.
As in *The World As Will and Idea*, the will of the self is a
part of the whole of will, the universal will of being. Stevens
calls it "the will of necessity, the will of wills." The effect

[14] *Will and Idea*, p. 277.

of the will is manifested as movement and changing appearance[15] and often figuratively presented as music. In "Notes toward a Supreme Fiction" the west wind on a pond is both an instance of will and a form of music: "The west wind was the music, the motion, the force" and "a will to change." The image (following Stevens' usual method with synecdoche) hovers between a factual meaning and a symbolic one by which a detail of the universal principle of being symbolizes that principle. The wind making its tiny frettings on the blank surface of a pond is both instance and symbol of the will creating and presenting the volatile world through change and movement; for "there was a will to change," and that is the present and necessary way that being is achieved.

Music, running the scale of meaning between the ordinary sense of the word and its symbolic senses, is Stevens' most pervasive figure. Like the air or tune played in "The Man with the Blue Guitar,"[16] it symbolizes the world as it is for the musician: not things as they are but things as they seem to him. This significance for music is carried by several other images of the player with his instrument. The analogy is extended even to its logical conclusion, to an analogy between silence and nothingness. The nothingness of what has vanished into the past is figuratively defined as a silence in "The Green Plant": "Silence is a shape that has passed." There is also the conventional, non-symbolic sense of the

[15] Santayana regards the force of universal will as a manifestation of the flux. See *Realms of Being*, pp. 377-78.

[16] The brief twentieth poem of "The Man with the Blue Guitar" holds in the word *air* a possible threefold pun. Air is first a part and instance of the reality that is the sustenance of life—the air, for instance, that we breathe into the empty hollow of the self. It is the space, too, in which we live and move. Finally, it is the tune of his guitar, the personal life he lives made up of the intimacy of individual experience. As the music is an expression of the musician's individual sense of things, it is also the music of the individual will that is part of the in-itself of all things, part of the universal will that we conceive of as reality, the present existence of things. The air, then, is what we believe, as the poem hopes.

word, but silence is one image (if it can be called an image), one word, the connotations of which are always an echo of its meaning. For instance, the music played on its instrument by the figure on a tomb in "Burghers of Petty Death" is the blank final silence of non-being after total destruction—the music of nothingness:

> . . . an imperium of quiet,
> In which a wasted figure, with an instrument,
> Propounds blank final music.

Although here the music is only silence, the figure playing an instrument is an image which, like that of "The Man with the Blue Guitar," represents the individual will and its individual sense of the world. Stevens repeats the image with many variations in many poems. In "Jumbo" a humorous version of the image is jumbo himself, a personification of the universal will of being in the role of the player with his instrument, as though the primal will were a wind[17] that plays upon the phenomenal world, plucking the trees like strings:

> The trees were plucked like iron bars
> And jumbo, the loud general-large
> Singsonged and singsonged, wildly free.

The wind singsonging and plucking the trees identifies the will with the flux. The will is creator of the forms of things emerging in phenomena, and jumbo is the transformer of the world. Since the will is also the in-itself of everything, he is himself transformed by his own transformations:

> Who the transformer, himself transformed,
> Whose single being, single form
> Were their resemblances to ours?

[17] Neumann on wind as a traditional image of the creative force quotes the *Upanishads:* "As the wind blows, everything grows." *Origins and History,* I, p. 22.

The one will—"single being, single form"—is also reflected in the multiplicity of individual wills and individual forms. Jumbo is "the secondary man" (with "secondary" having the sense it had for Locke), for he is also the basis of the appearance of things in an individual sensibility. As "ancestor of Narcissus," he is the source of individual will, of the ego, for universal will is particularized in the self that conceives or looks at itself. Santayana, in "The Realm of Matter," describes the self as Narcissus and as having emerged out of the depth of natural process. He speaks of the long vegetable and animal evolution that is the source of the human consciousness: "until one day, in the person of Narcissus, attention is arrested on the form which the self lends to all nature, or wears in its own eyes."[18]

Stevens usually sets forth the idea of individual will in the figure of the musician creating in his music his individual sense of reality. An early version of this symbolic meaning for music occurs in "Peter Quince at the Clavier": "Music is feeling, then, not sound." Another musician is the singer representing any conceiving mind in "The Idea of Order at Key West," whose singing is the creation of the conceived world that is the human world. Both singer and guitarist project in song and on strings an intensely personal view of the scene of life. "Things as they are / Are changed upon the blue guitar," and for the singer or conceiving self "there never was a world for her / Except the one she sang and, singing, made." The singer walking by the sea creates her song from the sound of water (the will manifested in the flux of things). Her song is not a mere medley of human voice and phenomena. It is a creation of an individual will through the deliberate order of language in its utterance, word by word:

[18] *Realms of Being*, p. 223.

> The song and water were not medleyed sound
> Even if what she sang was what she heard,
> Since what she sang was uttered word by word.

Stevens in this great poem bases his symbolic use of the
singer on an idea of the nature of song that can be understood in terms of Schopenhauer's statement of the nature of
the lyric. Schopenhauer describes song as a combination of
"desire"—the element of personal appetency in all intense
experience—and an individual sensory response or "pure
perception of the surrounding presented." A song, by this
definition, is an expression of an intensely felt personal vision
of the world. Schopenhauer says that for the singer or pure
lyrist "the subjective disposition, the affection of the will,
imparts its own hue to the perceived surrounding, and con-
versely, the surroundings communicate the reflex of their
color to the will."[19]

The music of the singer is beyond the genius of inanimate
matter, for it is the music or order imposed by the will of the
individual consciousness, or, as the poet says in "To the One
of Fictive Music," "the music summoned by the birth / That
separates us from the wind and sea." This poem addresses
itself to a personification of the human mind in its conceptual function. Stevens' personification here is recognizably
the muse of the human imagination, with the word *imagination* taken in its broadest sense as the continual creation
of the world in the human consciousness. The principle of
music, Stevens says in "The Whole Man: Perspectives,
Horizons," is more than an art, more than an addition to
humanity, for it is "humanity itself, in other than human
form."[20] Stevens' music symbol, with its special import suggesting the world apprehended in experience, approximates

---

[19] *Will and Idea,* p. 261.
[20] *OP,* p. 233.

Schopenhauer's remark that "we might, therefore, just as well call the world embodied music as embodied will."[21]

If the will of the individual becomes embodied in his conception of reality, the common will of men is adumbrated in their common vision of things. The first poem of "It Must Give Pleasure," from "Notes toward a Supreme Fiction," carrying further this figure of will compared to music, sets forth the human vision of reality as choral or orchestral music. The merging of one voice or instrument in harmony with another points to the idea that the general human conception of the world is a harmony of one individual vision with that of another, all following an established conception as a chorus or orchestra follows a musical composition. Thus, the accustomed flow of consciousness is an established traditional vision of reality that is followed by all the individual minds in an accordance like that of a musical group. The joy of experience, according to the poem, is that of mingling one's own conceptions with those of all men and singing in unison the notes that explore the range of human perceptions:

> For companies of voices moving there,
> To find of sound the bleakest ancestor,
> To find of light a music issuing

In this poetry sun and music are major symbols for being and the will to be, with night and silence carrying all the implications of the absence of sunlight and sound. The image of the player and instrument connotes the individual realization of things in a personal experience. This complex of symbols that makes all experience of the world embodied music and makes of the sun instance and evidence of reality is linked in a brilliant simile in "Montrachet-le-Jardin," in which Stevens compares the sun in its rising and

[21] *Will and Idea*, p. 274.

augmentation to one note repeated by a musician on one
string, to the very absolute or essence of music:[22]

> The sun expands, like a repetition on
> One string, an absolute, not varying
>
> Toward an inaccessible, pure sound.

5

The idea of nothingness for Stevens is nearly always some
version of the proposition that there can be no object without
a subject. Many of the familiar poems have themes related
to the same proposition. "The Snow Man," for instance, is
"nothing himself," for he is not a subjectivity. "Wild Ducks,
People and Distances," to recall the opening of this chapter,
also states that living reality depends on the presence of the
living mind, "except for that be-misted one and apart from
her," except for unrealized objective reality that is only an
assumption embodied in an image like the woman or the
rock. The assumption, when expressed as the rock, is an
image of the support of existence:

> It is true that you live on this rock
> And in it. It is wholly you.

"The priest of nothingness," the philosopher, speaks these
lines from "This as Including That" and after speaking he is
gone, for "the iron settee is cold." But there must be a living
presence to realize the rock, the reality, even if it is only a fly
crawling where a man might have leaned; therefore, the
poem concludes, "A fly crawls on the balustrades." In this
poem it is just as Schopenhauer says: "And yet, the existence

---

[22] For the image of the sun as sound, there is, for comparison, an interesting passage by Viollet-le-Duc: "But we cannot hear the sun rise; how, then,
can a symphony create in the mind the same sensations which are produced
by this daily phenomenon? Why do we say every day; this bit of music is
ravishing brightness . . ." *Discourses on Architecture*, p. 12.

of this whole world remains ever dependent upon the first eye that opened, even if it were that of an insect."[23] The title, "This as Including That," implies that the subject includes the object and that the rock is the content of the mind ("It is wholly you") as well as its support. Thus, the image, for all its simplicity, is able to convey more than one kind of meaning.

The image of the rock illustrates Stevens' strategy with symbols.[24] The image is loose and shapeless but has specific sensory connotations. It stands for the most indefinable of words, for *reality*, and yet many of the poems that contain the symbol are, in effect, definitions of it. The poet gains in this way a variety of meaning by use of the same amorphous vehicle and indefinite import. The rock is obviously Stevens' most inclusive symbol, for held within the unity of this simple primary image is all that is actual and all that may be imagined, the particular that exists as well as the possible that may exist. "The rock is the habitation of the whole," as the poem entitled "The Rock" defines its dominant symbol. The image is obvious and readily available, for it is the archetypal image of belief in substance. The attributes that common experience associates with rock usually modify the image, as in Christian symbolism. Schopenhauer uses the rock to indicate enduring existence in the midst of the flux: "time is like an unceasing stream, and the present a rock on which the stream breaks itself, but does not carry away with it."[25] Whitehead presents rock as an example of "the true and real things which endure" and sees in its shape "the abstract of things which recur."[26] For Stevens the image has

[23] *Will and Idea*, p. 45.
[24] For a more extensive discussion of this image, see Ralph J. Mills, "Wallace Stevens: The Image of the Rock," *Wallace Stevens*, ed. Borroff. The perceptive essay is a basic document for the reader of Stevens.
[25] *Will and Idea*, p. 292.
[26] *Adventures of Ideas*, p. 46.

many possibilities, for as is true of the word *reality*, the image of the rock comprises everything that exists. One of these possibilities is Schopenhauer's present being of reality. Speaking of the image with this significance in mind, Stevens in "Credences of Summer" calls it "the rock of summer" to describe the certainty of present existence, the brightness and assurance of direct perception, repose in the moment of life, and the security self finds in the actual:

> It is the visible rock, the audible,
> The brilliant mercy of a sure repose,
> On this present ground, the vividest repose,
> Things certain sustaining us in certainty.

This image is the vehicle of a subtle metaphor that expresses the notion of a permanent basis of existence that is impenetrable to thought and on which all forms and events subsist. The rock also is the truth, as "Credences of Summer" maintains, probably meaning by *truth* the whole of things, as in Santayana's definition:

The truth properly means the sum of all true propositions, what omniscience would assert, the whole ideal system of qualities and relations which the world has exemplified or will exemplify.[27]

In Poem XXVI of "The Man with the Blue Guitar," the rock is defined as the place where man is, the world that is resonant with human thoughts and feelings. Even though a place, it is a place conceived, perhaps only the location of mind, a permanence from which thought is continually falling away in the flux of experience:

> The world washed in his imagination,
> The world was a shore, whether sound or form
>
> Or light, the relic of farewells,
> Rock, of valedictory echoings,

[27] *Realms of Being*, p. 402.

> To which his imagination returned,
> From which it sped, a bar in space. . . .

"How to Live. What to Do" elaborates the idea of the image and anticipates its final development. The man and the woman of this poem climb the rock until they leave behind the fictions of their culture—choristers, priests, voices—and standing to rest, they have left only the height of the rock and the cold wind. The inference might be that from this bare perspective, this absolute, they could not know how to live or what to do.

"The Rock," the last and most elaborate of the poems utilizing this image, presents it in three parts and from three viewpoints. In Part I the rock is a possible but unrealized fundament for conscious being, an abstraction like the idea of substance that in itself is a blank or nothingness. The fact that on this nothingness life has come to subsist suggests that human experience is like the fulfillment of a will to be, a desire that man's conception may cover the blank rock with leaves and blooms. Part II develops this image of conscious life, "the body quickened and the mind in root," in terms of vegetation and describes the rock as the base or ground of the impermanent in its round of seasons. The rock is a bareness below man's thought, the very barrenness that is the material that he must conceive of and conceive with. The barrenness vanishes under the efflorescence of language and its flowering in thought. "They bud the whitest eye," the poem says, thus indicating the blooming of consciousness; for here again, the vision and ego are identified: the eye and the *I* are one.

According to its title, "Forms of the Rock in a Night-Hymn," Part III, lists aspects of the rock as though recounted in a music that issues from the primal source of being ("Night-Hymn"); therefore, all the imagery of this section can be considered as projected from man's interior dark.

The compendium of things for which the rock is said to stand constitutes all the specifics of human experience. First, the rock is each of the specific details of each life from the emergence of the individual until his eventual terminal. "The rock is the habitation of the whole," the poem says in summation, and it lists air, stars, events, beginnings, endings, and the mind of man holding all of these things. Thus, the rock of this poem is the content of the mind, the object that is nothing without the subject, that, by its inclusion in the mind or subject, becomes the unity of the world.

The most ingenious poem on the rock is "That Which Cannot Be Fixed," the first of the twin poems called "Two Versions of the Same Poem." "That which cannot be fixed" is the flux that is also the ground of being. In the complex figurative account of the poem, it is first a sea, and in the introductory lines that sea is identified as the rock, "insolid rock." The organic imagery of the poem expresses a sense of secret and living energy in the heart of a body floating in an unknown ocean whose pulsing tide represents the creation and decreation of process by which the more and more of all that comes into existence becomes the less and less of that which is dissolved in the past:

> Only there is

> A beating and a beating in the centre of
> The sea, a strength that tumbles everywhere,

> Like more and more becoming less and less. . . .

The central figure of the poem is that of the womb of nature and its fetus ("sleep deep, good eel"). The figure is given in the depiction of a body lying in the water of a sea in the center of which there is a beating and beating like that of a heart. The poem asks if nature, the cosmic mother of creation myths, holds man, "swollen / With thought through which it cannot see." What he cannot see is reality in itself, reality unrealized: the natural cosmic mother or the rock.

X

The Poetry of Thought

When one says that the poetry of thought should be the supreme poetry and when one considers with what thought has been concerned throughout so many ages, the themes of supreme poetry are not hard to identify.[1] Stevens

1

Though now a minor passage in literary history, the imagist controversy made its point so thoroughly that idea has had no settled place in poetry since. New criticism (lately grown old) certainly insists on the something said in poetry, but it still seems questionable for a poem to be ratiocinative. Now as the stature of Wallace Stevens begins to show itself as above and apart from the disputes of his contemporaries, the place of abstraction in poetry must be sought, and on his terms; for in his work abstraction again becomes a major element in poetry.

Nearly everyone who writes about Stevens mentions the quasi-philosophical character of his poetry, and much of the

[1] *OP*, p. 188.

criticism of Stevens tends to turn into summaries and lists of
his ideas. Because of the expository character of this poetry,
preoccupation with its ideas is only natural. Some of Stevens'
ideas resemble familiar concepts like Bergson's constant
novelty of phenomena or William James' discrete reality or
Santayana's essences. But even then they are not developed
as arguments but are given unsupported as though they
existed in simple immediacy without need of dialectic. When
detached from its language and approximated in a summary,
an idea from a poem of Stevens may emerge as only a slight
hypothesis vanishing almost while spoken. Even when most
solid and formulated, his abstract statements are often too
much the common topics of philosophic writing to be valu-
able intrinsically as profundities or discoveries; yet, the poetry
uses them as an intrinsic part of its own freshness and
permanence and abundance.

Stevens plainly did not intend insignificance for his ideas.
He maintained that "a poem in which the poet has chosen
for his subject a philosophic theme should result in the
poem of poems," but he also categorically stated that he was
not interested in employing poetry as a medium for the
presentation of a philosophy. A great many of his poems
give an idea as an insight into the nature of the relationship
of mind and reality,[2] presented as an intuition that is both
gnomic and intelligible. As for Stevens' own view of the

---

[2] *Reality,* in Stevens' use of the word, may be the world supposed to be
antecedent in itself or the world created in the specific occurrence of
thought, including the thinker himself and his mind forming the thought.
Often the term offers the assumption that if the self is the central point of
a circle of infinite radius, then reality is the not-self, including all except the
abstract subjective center. Sometimes *reality* is used in the context of the
nominalist position—then the word denotes that which is actual and stands
as a phenomenal identity, the existent as opposed to the merely fancied.
Stevens usually means by *reality* an undetermined base on which a mind
constructs its personal sense of the world. Occasionally he will use the word
real as a term of approval, as a substitute for the word *true,* and, therefore,
no more than an expression of confidence.

nature of his experience of things, a final summary is in order as a basis for a discussion of the nature of these themes and their poetic significance.

The world of Stevens' poetry reflects the changes of the flux of experience. The common vision of poetry is usually that of an objective world whose changes are an effect of its own mechanism. Stevens' poetry envisions a world burgeoning in the flow of consciousness and created continually in his sense of it. Stevens finds the actual to be an intermutation of an outer reality and the life within; he knows it through an interpretation of the indeterminate course of perception that interpretation itself alters. The conventional implicit concept of the work of the artist assumes that he is a mere observer of things, and this concept is taken from the point of view of one looking out of the self at a world external to it, as though men stood behind their eyes like watchers behind windows. Stevens' mind is both participant and spectator, creator and observer of movement and variety. Thus, he distrusts set facts and finds the ultimate in the tentative. In "Description without Place" he uses the attributes of objects as indicating a state of consciousness, the "seeming" of the world of that occasion:

> The sun is an example. What it seems
> It is and in such seeming all things are.

Many poets name and assess physical forms and use the value and sense of specific things to give an effect like that of live perception. They try to gain for language the physical qualities of bodies, their solidity, their actuality. Substances, physical objects, for Stevens, are subject to the transformations of the flow of consciousness and are known in all its changing lights, movement of values, attitudes, preconceptions, purposes. Thus, forms and objects have a use beyond their mere identity as, for instance, to embody concepts and express the way the world seems in those situations in which they occur. An appearance of a thing is, therefore, both an indication of the nature of the thing and a reflection of the self of that instant. In "Description without Place" the poet speaks of

> The difference that we make in what we see
>
> And our memorials of that difference.

The continual shift of appearance, therefore, is an effect of the flux of experience and the changing perspectives of the changing self. For the world is seen from an occupied center, and the occupied center, as Santayana says, is always a transcendental and moral point of location that "moves wherever the animal moves."[3] The character of the perspective rearranges itself in relation to the active self, as in "July Mountain," for instance, in which there is only a momentary organization of reality—momentary because it surrounds a volatile center. The poem begins with a statement that consciousness exists by instants of intuition separated by various spans of inattention and exists most of all in the highly organized instants of music and poetry:

> We live in a constellation
> Of patches and of pitches,
> Not in a single world. . . .

The world is a multiple possibility and not a single or a fixed world because it is always organized around a self, is always relative to the motion and ferment of a transcendental and moral center. Santayana's thought fills out the highly compressed context of the poem: "For even if nature as a whole has no centre, every organism is a focus for its external and changing relations to the rest of the world, and is the centre of a dynamic cosmos relative to itself."[4] Stevens' cosmos is

---

[3] *Realms of Being,* p. 244.
[4] *Ibid.,* p. 245.

incipient as well as dynamic because each present instant is
the beginning of a new arrangement of the reality that each
subjective center realizes about itself:

> Thinkers without final thoughts
> In an always incipient cosmos,
> The way, when we climb a mountain,
> Vermont throws itself together.

A present instant of realization is a peak of summer or
"July Mountain," when reality assembles itself like the
spontaneous ordering of speech or the perfected arrangement
of art.[5]

2

Even from this brief account, it should be evident that
idea in Stevens has a poetic rather than a philosophic function. If Stevens' ideas are often undeveloped or trite or out-
worn, still the resemblance to philosophic writing is more
than fortuitous. The evidence of "A Collect of Philosophy"
is enough to support a suspicion that Stevens searched for
ideas that might be used as a base for poems. When a passage
of philosophic prose is placed beside a poem of Stevens the
similarities and differences emerge, especially when the ideas
in both are almost parallel. A passage useful as illustration
is by a philosopher who is also a poet, and for this reason the
language of the two works is closer together. It is not a tech-
nical passage, but still it is a philosophical passage and has

---

[5] The image of a spontaneous creation of order at the moment of realization is similar to some of the ideas and images of "Connoisseur of Chaos,"
especially the famous image of the eagle "for which the intricate Alps are a
single nest." The paradoxes in the beginning of this poem, "a violent order
is disorder" and "a great disorder is an order," are propositions that, in one
form or another, are implicit in a great deal of Stevens' work. Alexander, in
Space, Time and Deity, p. 237, has an equivalent observation: "But system
in general exists in every complex, even in the least organized; all disorder
has its own complex plan."

the advantage of being almost as self-contained as a poem. Santayana is describing the effect of the intuition of an essence on the self:

> The important point, however, is not how intuition is reached, but that when reached it reveals an essence belonging of itself neither here nor there, but undated and eternal. Such essences are set over against existence everywhere and at all times, and it remains for existence, if it will, to embody their forms or to give attention to them, so that they may become evident to living spirits. And a living spirit finds a great joy in conceiving them, but because in conceiving them it is liberated from the pressure of ulterior things, energizes perfectly, and simply conceives.[6]

"Martial Cadenza" is an intuition of an essence, "undated and eternal," without time, caught in an integration of experience. Although the word *martial* in the title may refer to the image of the silent armies of the second stanza, it conveys some of the effect of a bravery, a soldierly flourish in the face of oncoming time. The poem abstracts an evanescence, the present, into an essence that is a permanence, the point of unvarying light of the moment of consciousness like the star that is its image:

> Only this evening I saw again low in the sky
> The evening star, at the beginning of winter. . . .

Winter and evening in all these poems bear their burden of traditional connotations for age and approaching death, but the star is constant; it recurs "as if life came back," he feels, seeing it shining again. In its recurrence, life recurs,

> . . . as if it came back, as if life came back,
> Not in a later son, a different daughter, another place,
> But as if evening found us young, still young,
> Still walking in a present of our own.

[6] *Essays in Literary Criticism of George Santayana,* ed. Irving Singer (New York, 1956), p. 245.

In the light shining there an embodiment of an essence occurs, and by it the present is transformed into the eternal. As the eternal is a world without time, it is like something without being, "an essence belonging of itself neither here nor there," either because it is without factual existence or because it has existence no longer in the sense that past experiences have no existence since memory does not constitute an existence of the actual experience:

> It was like sudden time in a world without time,
> This world, this place, the street in which I was,
> Without time: as that which is not has no time,
> Is not, or is of what there was. . . .

Then he thinks of the world of the past, that world abandoned by time, and in one of his supreme fictions, he realizes the silence of non-being and sees the dead world of past occurrence stilled in absolute vanquishment:

>   . . . full
> Of the silence before the armies, armies without
> Either trumpets or drums, the commanders mute, the arms
> On the ground, fixed fast in a profound defeat.

With only the wisp of a memory of Matthew Arnold's ignorant armies or even of Keats' steadfast star, he sees his star again as a form of time itself, with time conceived of as that moment in which all reality exists, the eternal moment of being, reality in itself and apart from any mere temporary and individual consciousness:

>   . . . Itself
> Is time, apart from any past, apart
> From any future, the ever-living and being,
> The ever-breathing and moving, the constant fire. . . .

The star is the constant presence of the present, the eternal moment of an existent reality that is always there:

> The vivid thing in the air that never changes,
> Though the air change. . . .

He sees it as a central reality—an essence, not a symbol—and in his realization he becomes one with that fire. He flashes again as it flashes. Thus, by a conjunction of opposites, the fragile temporary *I* is identified with the eternal vivid moment of time, the point of living present. In that identity the self, the living spirit of Santayana's passage, realizing this essence, "energizes perfectly, and simply conceives."

> . . . Only this evening I saw it again,
> As the beginning of winter, and I walked and talked
> Again, and lived and was again, and breathed again
> And moved again and flashed again, time flashed again.

Although Santayana's prose is closer to poetry than is usual for philosophy and Stevens' poems are correspondingly closer to philosophic statement than poetry usually is, the profound breach between them becomes plainer by their similarities. The obvious differences between the two—between the direct assertion of mere statement, of the voice speaking straight to the receiving mind; and the implications of the fictive statement, of the voice speaking in a situation, a condition of a place and a time, "this world, this place, the street in which I was"—these differences, enhanced by the different rhythmic effects of the passage of prose and of the poem, are the contrasting appearances of the two; but it is the subterranean root system of human experience of the poem that makes it a burgeoning tree to the simple monument of the prose. For instance, Santayana means to say precisely what he says, but Stevens implies a secret and poignant denial of his conjunction of self and star. The poem expresses his sense of exaltation at this embodiment of the concept of eternity as the moment of living experience. That is what he says, openly and longingly. But there to deny the union of the self and the image of eternity are his silent, defeated armies, instances of that mortal world with which his poem must cope.

We face here an instance of the intricate function of the fictive element in poetry. The fictive element in a philosophic passage consists of no more than the occasion of its utterance. In a poem, however, there is the presence of an implied and often intense human situation, and there are the purposes of the poem itself, fulfilled in its fictive character. The fictive aspect of poetry invades the normally simple and candid nature that a plain statement of an idea usually has. The ideas in Stevens' poems participate in the fictive character of the poem, especially in that they give the whole poem the guise of a moment of insight or realization or of an affirmation of belief. These ideas avoid the question of their truth value by their participation in the fictive.

It is important to remember that a statement, even an abstract one, cannot avoid a source of some kind for its words, an uttering voice with some sort of an occasion. Stevens' ideas are enveloped by the inevitable circumstances of language, the voice, and its situation. Therefore, what we have is either more or less of a fictive action. The action can be fairly overt, as in "Martial Cadenza," in which the speaker is in a specific place, his street, with the conflict of his mortality and his yearning for permanence; or the poem may hold no more than the elemental vestigial situation, the instance of utterance. A philosophic idea seems to hold aloof from the vestigial situation of a philosophic passage; and a poetic idea, to engage in that situation, in fact to amplify it. In a great many of Stevens' poems, his ideas, like the slight action usual in most lyrics, provide a surface for immediate attention and give the poem a guise or a role to perform. This guise for Stevens is that of an intuition of reality; thus, idea carries on for him a function for the whole poem that

resembles the function of an action in a poem with a dominant dramatic character. His poetic ideas engage us in a
semblance of an experience that is specific in character and
expresses a certain individual sense of the world. And when
abstracted for purposes of study, that is what they mainly
seem to do. The abstraction of ideas from poetry is an awk-
ward but useful critical device that gives only a rough
approximation of the cognitive material. Getting at this abstract content as best we can, in time it shows itself as a
means of approaching intense experience in living, for
Stevens uses his ideas almost as another poet would use a
dramatic content. In this way Stevens' use of idea often in-
verts the usual relationship of experience and idea in a poem.
We are accustomed to poems in which a fiction, an invented
situation or a particular mode of action, becomes a representation of an abstraction by standing as symbolic of an
idea, or as part and instance of a universal. Thus, the speci-
fied thing or event, transformed by implication, is turned
into a general concept. Stevens' poems are often made of this
traditional experience-into-cognition arrangement; but just
as often he reverses it with an arrangement of idea into
experience.

Any idea, the transforming idea of a poem or the literal
idea of expository prose, bears as an inherent flaw the difficulty of its acceptance by a reader. We accept an action as
performing the functions of the fictive and do not demand
historicity of it in the way that we demand verity of an idea.
But an idea in a poem is inextricably mingled with the
human situation in which it exists and in which it is
imagined. By no means, however, does the fictive element
impugn the poet's sincerity; yet, it would be naïve to abstract
an idea from a poem and ask whether or not the poet believes
in it. First of all, an idea thus abstracted from a poem is a
critic's hypothesis and never identical to the idea in the poem.

Ideas are truly offered only according to their use and presentation in the poem, and by this particular presentation the poet defines his position in relation to these ideas. When the ideas of a poem are presented as though they had truth value and not as the mere expression of a role, the poem has the effect of a personal affirmation. Unlike a philosophic statement, the truth value of an affirmation in poetry does not require a logical justification but depends on elements that gain simple and universal acceptance like those that are an abstraction of evident and common human experience.

Here it should be repeated that Stevens himself insists on the value of his ideas, but he also insists that this truth value exist only in the particular sense of existence given in one of his poems; for the kind of truth value that an idea in a poem by Stevens normally has is intuitive and revelatory rather than practical and applicable beyond the context. His realizations or "secretions of insight," as Stevens calls them, embody experience as though the idea created special circumstances in which the world could be known but only in a certain way and according to the terms of the idea itself. The idea of "On the Road Home" has such a function. Its contrast of the old philosophic pair, the one and the many, is no more than a simple rejection of one and vindication of the other in terms of a new realization of living, a result of his awareness of the vividness and particularity of immediate experience:

> It was when I said,
> "There is no such thing as the truth,"
> That the grapes seemed fatter.
> The fox ran out of his hole.

This is that fox who, now turned pluralist, finds the grapes of reality no longer sour. Was it not truth, that most fabulous of ideas, this same bare unrealized thought, that Keats found one with beauty, thereby conjoining the ultimate in abstraction with the ultimate in experience?

> You . . . You said,
> "There are many truths,
> But they are not parts of a truth."

Whoever the "you" may have been, William James, writing in *Pragmatism* about *the* truth, saw it dissolved into the pluralism of the specific items of the moment of consciousness: "For pluralistic pragmatism, truth grows up inside of all the finite experiences. They lean on each other, but the whole of them, if such a whole there be, leans on nothing. All 'homes' are in finite experience; finite experience as such is homeless. Nothing outside of the flux secures the issue of it. It can hope salvation only from its own intrinsic promises and potencies."[7] It was in "On the Road Home" that Stevens says that he became aware that anything real is individual and exists only in a particular experience of it. Thus it is that pluralism gives the real things within the flux, and man standing in that flux stands alone. Then, in that realization, the tree becomes an experience and the real (the green) becomes the blue (the conceived):

> Then the tree, at night, began to change,
>
> Smoking through green and smoking blue.
> We were two figures in a wood.
> We said we stood alone.

Introducing truth as an almost sacred idea to monists—one of the idols of the tribe of men—William James finds it a mere form of speech, unlike the pluralism that he conceives as made up of the particulars of consciousness: "What hardens the heart of everyone I approach with the view of truth sketched in my last lecture [truth as relation among the details of experience] is that typical idol of the tribe, the notion of *the* Truth, conceived as the one answer, determinate and complete to the one fixed enigma which the world

[7] P. 169.

is believed to propound." At another time he says, "*The* Truth: what a perfect idol of the rationalistic mind!"[8] Stevens, too, finds *the* truth falsely enshrined; and finding reality in the idea of pluralism, like a poet but unlike a philosopher, he turns it into a way of regarding the world, and the idea is dissolved in an experience:

> It was when you said,
> "The idols have seen lots of poverty,
> Snakes and gold and lice,
> But not the truth";
>
> It was at that time, that the silence was largest
> And longest, the night was roundest,
> The fragrance of the autumn warmest,
> Closest and strongest.

Although there is some appearance of a source for Stevens' poem in "Pragmatism and Humanism," from which these passages by James are extracted, conjunction of the poetry and prose is made in order to exhibit the different functions of a similar idea in each. James' discussion is a contributing one, a tributary of his main stream of argument; for he goes on to show that pragmatism is pluralistic, and he raises the old philosophic dispute of the one and the many in order to define the position of pragmatism and to oppose the position of rationalism. Stevens, using the same dispute, takes his pluralism as a way of seeing the world. He does not reinforce any larger theory of pragmatism or of anything else. Pluralism is an intuition of reality in Stevens' poem. The abstract element becomes the poet's means of certain realizations. To turn to the poem's last two stanzas, silence for Stevens has implications of non-being and of a universe indifferent to

---

[8] *Ibid.*, p. 157. By "idol of the tribe" James refers to the section on idols in Bacon's *Novum Organum*. Bacon characterizes inherent human misjudgments as idols of the tribe. Stevens apparently uses the word *idols* in its conventional sense.

man, and it was at that moment of grasping plurality and seeing the idols, in association with immediate human experience rather than rationalistic Truth, that this silence becomes "largest and longest." In contrast with that silence, he enters intensely his own immediate sense of the round night and the warm fragrant autumn.

Obviously the ideas of a philosophic passage tend toward concatenation. Stevens' ideas are independent realizations even when the poem is only a part of a larger composition. Thus devoid of a logical basis, his ideas appear under the guise of intuition. Also, the special qualities of the language of the prose are of minor importance, but Stevens' ideas live only in the specific conditions of language and feeling of the poem. Poetry has an incantatory quality that suggests a revelatory or intuitive meaning, and intuition is the traditional import of poetry. The intuition of a poem of Stevens is both an outward and an inward regard. It is a realization of the world that in its abstractness, unsupported by the special pleading of logic, gives an effect of objective and immediate vision. In "Angel Surrounded by Paysans" Stevens' own personification of intuition, his necessary angel of reality, says:

> . . . in my sight, you see the earth again,
>
> Cleared of its stiff and stubborn, man-locked set,
> And, in my hearing, you hear its tragic drone
>
> Rise liquidly in liquid lingerings,
> Like watery words awash; like meanings said
>
> By repetitions of half-meanings.

This very realization is inevitably the poet's personal expression, existing only in the individual verbal form of the poem. For one of Stevens' generation and interests, it would be difficult to speak of intuition without some attention to the emphasis on intuition in philosophy at the turn of the century. The poems of Stevens remind us of the intuition of Bergson in that many of these poems are an insight into an aspect of reality by the self, an intuition of an object by a subject; and they remind us of Croce in that they are, too, an expression of that unique self and represent the poet's sense of the world in his own individual language form. Thus, inasmuch as a poem of Stevens is composition as realization, it is a Bergsonian intuition, and it becomes at the same time a Crocean intuition in that it is composition as expression. Obviously, any poem may be an intuition according to Croce's meaning; the Bergsonian sense of the term is more restrictive. The poetry of Stevens achieves the status of an intuition according to both interpretations of the word.

It would be a mistake, however, to look to Bergson or Croce or Santayana or anyone else for a specific source here. Stevens does not go into the matter enough to make a search for philosophical affinities worthwhile; in fact, he never goes into any of his ideas, especially the ideas in his poems, far enough to relate him other than as an eclectic reader. These ideas of his have other purposes than philosophic ones and are really only half ideas after all. Stevens in his poetic wisdom never made them more.

The secret of the effect of these ideas is their lack of elaboration. Stevens' usual plan for cognition in a poem is to use an abstraction as an over-all expository scheme and then within that scheme to move from one idea to another, these contained ideas being almost discrete and used to support the emotional implications of the major ideas rather than to express abstract import. In other words, his subsidiary ideas do not elaborate the over-all idea; they elaborate its emotional implications. Stevens is too knowing a poet to subject his poems to an overwhelming cognitive content. What appears to be an elaboration of an idea may only be the repetition of its slight meaning.

To show Stevens' ideas as only "meanings said / By repetitions of half-meanings," a poem and a passage of philosophy will again be placed in juxtaposition. The two contexts have such similar ideas that one could almost be used to explain the other.

There is a dramatic passage in Francis Herbert Bradley's *Appearance and Reality* that follows a long skeptical introduction discrediting all objective evidence of reality. After almost 150 pages in which he reduces apparent reality to the status of mere appearance, he suddenly affirms his belief that reality is made of feeling and experience:

> I will state the case briefly thus. Find any piece of existence, take up anything that anyone could possibly call a fact, or could in any sense assert to have being, and then judge if it does not consist in sentient experience. Try to discover any sense in which you can still continue to speak of it, when all perception and feeling have been removed; or point out any fragment of its matter, any aspect of its being, which is not derived from and is still not relative to this source. When the experiment is made strictly, I can myself conceive of nothing else than the experienced. Anything, in no sense felt or perceived, becomes to me quite unmeaning. And as I cannot try to think of it without realizing either that I am not thinking at all, or that I am thinking of it against my will as being experienced, I am driven to the conclusion that for me experience is the same as reality.[9]

Remember from this passage that anything, any piece of existence, even a fact, must consist of sentient experience, that the existent cannot exist without perception and feeling, that "experience is the same as reality," and then turn to Part II of Stevens' "Holiday in Reality":

[9] London, 1939, pp. 127–28.

The flowering Judas grows from the belly or not at all.
The breast is covered with violets. It is a green leaf.
Spring is umbilical or else it is not spring.
Spring is the truth of spring or nothing, a waste, a fake.
These trees and their argentines, their dark-spiced
    branches,
Grow out of the spirit or they are fantastic dust.
The bud of the apple is desire, the down-falling gold,
The catbird's gobble in the morning half-awake—
These are real only if I make them so. Whistle
For me, grow green for me and, as you whistle and grow
    green,
Intangible arrows quiver and stick in the skin
And I taste at the root of the tongue the unreal of
    what is real.

The obvious thing about these two quotations is what was mentioned in relation to James and Stevens. Bradley's is a small part of a long work with a remarkable continuity and unity, and the idea of his passage quoted above is only a fragment of his elaborate abstract structure. He qualifies and defines this element of his thinking, building to it and beyond it his intricate argument. Taken alone it would have strong implications for Bradley's thought, implications that he hastens to correct, such as its suggestion of solipsism. And all its implications are cognitive ones.

Stevens' passage is a whole poem, an integer. The first part of "Holiday in Reality," which is not quoted here, is, in fact, another separate poem, with a separate idea. Stevens takes this bare concept, the identity of reality and sentient experience, and makes his poem out of its repetition. His expression of his idea is a paean of amazement almost, an utterance with a certain feeling and manner, intent upon the way this idea seems and upon the way reality seems in this idea. It is certainly not a prayer, but it does have some qual-

ities of reverence. It has implications, but they are implications of feeling rather than of cognition. These implications
pertain to a certain quality of being and particular forms of
experience. The cognitive and logical implications of this
fragment of idea are of minor consequence in the poem. To
pursue them would be to leave the poem for one's own
speculation.

What we have in Stevens' poem is an idea that, in its own
proper native language, functions as a vehicle of particular
experience itself. With "I taste at the root of the tongue the
unreal of what is real," Stevens is giving the intuition of his
poetry, not an intuition of a particular thing but a particular
intuition, and one of that reality that is indistinguishably
both mind and world.

In the common sense, intuition leans toward an apperception of specifics and away from abstract concepts; but the
intuition in Stevens' poetry is an idea that gives a particular
sense of the world, and its specifics are those of a certain
integration of experience. Although this integration is gained
through an abstraction, even one that is only the slightest
kind of an idea, it contains something of the drama of being
and of a specific existence. It does not have to contain a
listing of specifics, an itemization of single certain forms or
even of single certain moments. It itself is a single certain
experience.

As a matter of fact, the specific items and specific images
in Stevens' poem are generic ones: the flowering Judas is any
flowering Judas; the breast and its violets are any breast and
its violets. More than that, these generic images are transformed into larger abstractions, and the breast and its violets
become sentience and its created reality. Thus, even while
grasping for their specificity, these apparent items expand
into vast and simple abstractions. The one most particular
thing here is the individual experience, the "I taste at the
root of the tongue." What is it, then, that is tasted there but
the whole unbounded content of experience?

⟨⟩ INDEX OF POEMS ⟨⟩

Poems from *Opus Posthumous* are indicated by *OP*. Poems from *The Necessary Angel* are indicated by *NA*. All other poems in the index below are from *The Collected Poems of Wallace Stevens*.

217

INDEX OF NAMES AND TITLES

221

STEVENS' POETRY OF THOUGHT

by Frank Doggett

Designer:	Cecilie Smith
Typesetter:	Baltimore Type and Composition Corporation
Typefaces:	Baskerville (text), Bulmer (display)
Printer:	The Murray Printing Company
Paper:	Lindenmeyr Schlosser Company
Binder:	William Marley Company (cloth edition)
	The Murray Printing Company (paperback edition)

5110